Illegal Drug Use

ISSUES

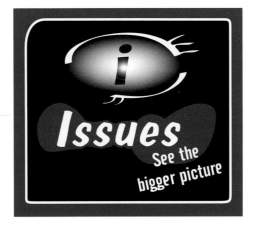

Volume 228

Series Editor

Lisa Firth

Independence

Educational Publishers

First published by Independence

The Studio, High Green

Great Shelford

Cambridge CB22 5EG

England

© Independence 2012

British Library Cataloguing in Publication Data

Illegal drug use. -- (Issues ; v. 228)

1. Drug abuse--Great Britain. 2. Drugs of abuse--Law and

legislation--Great Britain.

I. Series II. Firth, Lisa.

362.2'9-dc23

ISBN-13: 978 1 86168 617 6

Printed in Great Britain

MWL Print Group Ltd

CONTENTS

Chapter 1 Illegal Drugs in the UK

Overview of the UK drug scene   1

If someone who has taken drugs...   2

Drugs   3

Ketamine problems on the rise   5

'Safe ketamine': experts warn over trend for 'legal high' drug   6

Introduction to solvent and volatile substance abuse   7

Cannabis and schizophrenia   8

'Cannabis cure for brain cancer' headline is misleading   9

Amy Winehouse's death prompts compulsory drug education in schools campaign   10

Clever children more likely to take drugs   11

Chapter 2 The Effects of Drug Abuse

The effects and impacts of drugs   12

Dependent drug users   13

How to recognise drug abuse   14

Drug treatment in England: the road to recovery   16

'The story of what made me who I am'   19

Chapter 3 Drugs and the Law

Illegal drug use in the UK   21

Drug policy: legislation, strategies and economic analysis   24

Sentencing guideline for drug offences comes into force   28

Deal or new deal? How the designer drugs trade impacts UK classification laws   32

Drugs – time for better laws   34

Illegal drug use is in decline, NHS figures reveal   35

Call for action on 'legal high' drugs   36

Getting tough on drugs just doesn't work   39

Key Facts   40

Glossary   41

Index   42

Acknowledgements   43

Assignments   44

OTHER TITLES IN THE ISSUES SERIES

For more on these titles, visit: www.independence.co.uk

The Internet Revolution ISBN 978 1 86168 451 6
An Ageing Population ISBN 978 1 86168 452 3
Poverty and Exclusion ISBN 978 1 86168 453 0
Waste Issues ISBN 978 1 86168 454 7
Staying Fit ISBN 978 1 86168 455 4
The AIDS Crisis ISBN 978 1 86168 468 4
Bullying Issues ISBN 978 1 86168 469 1
Marriage and Cohabitation ISBN 978 1 86168 470 7
Privacy and Surveillance ISBN 978 1 86168 472 1
The Animal Rights Debate ISBN 978 1 86168 473 8
Body Image and Self-Esteem ISBN 978 1 86168 484 4
Abortion – Rights and Ethics ISBN 978 1 86168 485 1
Racial and Ethnic Discrimination ISBN 978 1 86168 486 8
Sexual Health ISBN 978 1 86168 487 5
Selling Sex ISBN 978 1 86168 488 2
Citizenship and Participation ISBN 978 1 86168 489 9
Health Issues for Young People ISBN 978 1 86168 500 1
Reproductive Ethics ISBN 978 1 86168 502 5
Tackling Child Abuse ISBN 978 1 86168 503 2
Money and Finances ISBN 978 1 86168 504 9
The Housing Issue ISBN 978 1 86168 505 6
Teenage Conceptions ISBN 978 1 86168 523 0
Work and Employment ISBN 978 1 86168 524 7
Understanding Eating Disorders ISBN 978 1 86168 525 4
Student Matters ISBN 978 1 86168 526 1
Cannabis Use ISBN 978 1 86168 527 8
Health and the State ISBN 978 1 86168 528 5
Tobacco and Health ISBN 978 1 86168 539 1
The Homeless Population ISBN 978 1 86168 540 7
Coping with Depression ISBN 978 1 86168 541 4
The Changing Family ISBN 978 1 86168 542 1
Bereavement and Grief ISBN 978 1 86168 543 8
Endangered Species ISBN 978 1 86168 544 5
Responsible Drinking ISBN 978 1 86168 555 1
Alternative Medicine ISBN 978 1 86168 560 5
Censorship Issues ISBN 978 1 86168 558 2
Living with Disability ISBN 978 1 86168 557 5
Sport and Society ISBN 978 1 86168 559 9
Self-Harming and Suicide ISBN 978 1 86168 556 8
Sustainable Transport ISBN 978 1 86168 572 8
Mental Wellbeing ISBN 978 1 86168 573 5
Child Exploitation ISBN 978 1 86168 574 2
The Gambling Problem ISBN 978 1 86168 575 9
The Energy Crisis ISBN 978 1 86168 576 6
Nutrition and Diet ISBN 978 1 86168 577 3
Coping with Stress ISBN 978 1 86168 582 7
Consumerism and Ethics ISBN 978 1 86168 583 4

Genetic Modification ISBN 978 1 86168 584 1
Education and Society ISBN 978 1 86168 585 8
The Media ISBN 978 1 86168 586 5
Biotechnology and Cloning ISBN 978 1 86168 587 2
International Terrorism ISBN 978 1 86168 592 6
The Armed Forces ISBN 978 1 86168 593 3
Vegetarian Diets ISBN 978 1 86168 594 0
Religion in Society ISBN 978 1 86168 595 7
Tackling Climate Change ISBN 978 1 86168 596 4
Euthanasia and Assisted Suicide ISBN 978 1 86168 597 1
A Sustainable Future ISBN 978 1 86168 603 9
Class and Social Mobility ISBN 978 1 86168 604 6
Population Growth and Migration ISBN 978 1 86168 605 3
Equality and Gender Roles ISBN 978 1 86168 606 0
Tourism and Travel ISBN 978 1 86168 607 7
Crime, Punishment and Justice ISBN 978 1 86168 608 4
Domestic and Relationship Abuse ISBN 978 1 86168 613 8
LGBT Equality ISBN 978 1 86168 614 5
Globalisation and Trade ISBN 978 1 86168 615 2
Ethics in Business ISBN 978 1 86168 616 9
Illegal Drug Use ISBN 978 1 86168 617 6
Protecting Human Rights ISBN 978 1 86168 618 3

A note on critical evaluation

Because the information reprinted here is from a number of different sources, readers should bear in mind the origin of the text and whether the source is likely to have a particular bias when presenting information (just as they would if undertaking their own research). It is hoped that, as you read about the many aspects of the issues explored in this book, you will critically evaluate the information presented. It is important that you decide whether you are being presented with facts or opinions. Does the writer give a biased or an unbiased report? If an opinion is being expressed, do you agree with the writer?

Illegal Drug Use offers a useful starting point for those who need convenient access to information about the many issues involved. However, it is only a starting point. Following each article is a URL to the relevant organisation's website, which you may wish to visit for further information.

Overview of the UK drug scene

Information from DrugScope.

There is a common perception that drug use in the UK is out of control – that all young people take drugs and that drug use and dealing is rampant across Britain's playgrounds. The facts suggest otherwise, but as with many misconceptions, there are elements of truth: the UK regularly features at or near the top of any Euro league of drug use among young people and it would be ridiculous to categorically deny that drugs are in circulation in any school. However, a combination of official statistics, academic research and DrugScope's own information sources on the ground present a much more mixed and complex picture.

How many people use drugs?

Of the general adult population aged 16–59, around ten million people, or 30%, say they have ever tried an illegal drug. The figure drops to around 10% for use in the last year and just over 5% for use in the last month.

For those aged 16–24, the main age group likely to be using drugs on a more regular basis, over 20% said they had used a drug in the last month.

For those aged 11–15, around 22% said they had used a drug at least once; 15% in the last year and 8% in the last month.

What have been the main trends in use in recent years?

For all age groups, cannabis is far and away the most popular drug, whether you are talking about a once-in-a-lifetime experiment or regular use. Cannabis use has been falling in recent years.

Overall, drug use has either fallen or remained stable in the past ten years.

The only drug that showed a significant rise in use in the late nineties and early noughties was cocaine powder. Even that seemed to level off, then took a jump among those aged 16–24 for reasons which were unclear, before dipping again.

After cannabis, cocaine has become the second drug of choice, leapfrogging over amphetamine and ecstasy.

So-called 'legal highs' (a number of which are now banned, like mephedrone) have been hitting the headlines. While use appears to be widespread, these drugs have yet to figure in official statistics so it is hard to get an idea of exactly how many people are using them. However, it seems likely that the Internet will play an increasing role in drug information, manufacture and distribution.

How much does drug use cost the UK?

The drugs that cause most harm to the individual, families and the wider community are heroin and crack. These drugs account for most of the cost of drug treatment and drug enforcement and are the drugs most likely to generate crime in order to fund drug purchase. Therefore, cost estimates are largely based on use and supply of these drugs. There have been two studies – one for England and Wales and the other for Scotland. The combined estimated cost came to nearly £19 billion.

Ambulance

NOT THE SORT OF TRIP SHE HAD HOPED FOR!

How much does the UK spend dealing with the problem?

The latest data is from 2008/09. Out of a total labelled spend of £998 million, roughly two-thirds was spent on health and one-third on enforcement, with a very small amount (about 0.4% of the budget) spent on education. However, the published figures significantly under-estimate the costs of enforcement. This is because the money spent on drug enforcement is wrapped up in the overall budget for tackling organised crime and is therefore hard to tease out. The Serious Organised Crime Agency (SOCA) has an annual budget of around £400 million.

How many people have a drug dependency?

It is estimated that there are around 400,000 people in the UK with a dependency on heroin and/or crack. Of those, around half are in contact with treatment services.

How many people die because of drugs?

In 2009, coroners deemed that the deaths of 2,182 people in the UK were drug-related. 72% were classed as accidental poisoning or overdose, 9% were deemed to be suicide while the exact circumstances of the remaining fatalities remained unclear. Nearly 70% of drug-related deaths (around 1,400) involved heroin, methadone or similar opiate drugs.

By comparison, in 2008, just under 10,000 people died from alcohol-related diseases and over 100,000 people died from tobacco-related diseases.

How many people commit drug offences?

In 2008/09, there were nearly 300,000 recorded drug crimes in the UK, around 200,000 of which were warnings about possession of cannabis. The number of cocaine powder offences jumped 24% from the previous year.

How many drugs are seized by police and customs?

The most noticeable recent trend has been the increase in the number of cannabis plants seized, due to the number of cannabis farms discovered. Generally, it is customs who seize the largest amount of drugs in weight, while the police make the biggest number of individual seizures.

⇨ The above information is reprinted with kind permission from DrugScope. Visit www.drugscope.org. uk for more information.

© DrugScope 2011

If someone has taken drugs...

Gets really drowsy

⇨ Calm them and be reassuring.

⇨ NEVER give coffee to rouse them.

⇨ If symptoms persist, place them in the recovery position.

⇨ Call an ambulance if necessary.

Gets tense and panics

⇨ Calm them and be reassuring.

⇨ Explain that the feelings will pass.

⇨ Steer them clear of crowds, noisy music and bright lights.

⇨ If they start breathing very quickly, calm them down and encourage them to take long, slow breaths.

Gets too hot and dehydrates

⇨ Move them to a cooler, quiet area (outside is often best).

⇨ Remove excess clothing and try to cool them down.

⇨ Encourage them to sip non-alcoholic fluids such as fruit juice and isotonic sports drinks (about a pint every hour).

⇨ If symptoms persist call an ambulance, but make sure someone stays with them.

Ecstasy and speed affect the body's temperature control. If users dance energetically without taking regular breaks or keeping up fluids, there's a real danger that their bodies could overheat and dehydrate (lose too much body fluid). Warning signs include: cramps, fainting, headache or sudden tiredness.

Becomes unconscious

⇨ Call an ambulance.

⇨ Place them in the recovery position.

⇨ Check breathing. Be prepared to do mouth-to-mouth resuscitation.

⇨ Keep them warm, but not too hot.

If you've called an ambulance and know what drugs have been taken, always tell the crew. It might save a life and you won't get into trouble.

⇨ Information from Surgery Door. Visit www. surgerydoor.co.uk for more information.

© Surgery Door

DRUGSCOPE

Drugs

Information from the University of Cambridge Counselling Service.

A desire to experience an altered state of consciousness has been a feature of human culture from time immemorial. In the search for mood- and mind-altering substances, humankind has long experimented and taken risks.

Perhaps more than ever before, we are surrounded by legal drugs in coffee, alcohol and cigarettes, let alone in prescribed medications such as sleeping tablets, tranquillisers and opioid painkillers. Using these can be a temptingly easy way to change or control one's mood and psychological state. Advertising and marketing may enhance the appeal of substance use. There are fashions in drug use and the use of a certain drug may be associated with a particular (and perhaps desirable) lifestyle or subculture.

It is likely that you will encounter illicit drug use either prior to or at university. It is estimated that at least 60% of students will have tried cannabis at some time or another. About 33% will experiment with other substances. In a survey of Cambridge University students carried out between 1995 and 1998, 10% reported using cannabis on a weekly basis and 30% at some point during the previous year. Between 3% and 7% reported using other drugs such as ecstasy and amphetamines in the previous year. The majority of occasional users come to no long-term harm. They are also unlikely to harm others. Inevitably, some will run into problems, and, more seriously, some risk death as a direct result of their drug use.

Substances used

Recreational drugs can be classified as stimulants, depressants and hallucinogens. Some drugs, however, can overlap these categories: for example, ecstasy is both a stimulant and a hallucinogen, and, while low-grade cannabis (hash) works as a depressant, stronger versions such as skunk may also have hallucinogenic properties.

Stimulants

Stimulants work by increasing neural activity in the brain. They have the short-term effect of making one feel lively, talkative, confident and euphoric. They are attractive to club- and party-goers because they enhance sensory experience and postpone the need for sleep. As their effect wears off, however, they can leave you feeling restless, irritable or washed out. There may, therefore, be a temptation to avoid these 'coming down' feelings by taking more of the drug.

Long-term use or high doses can lead to extreme agitation, insomnia, delusions, hallucinations and paranoia, particularly in susceptible individuals.

The most common stimulants are:

⇨ Amphetamines (speed)

⇨ Ecstasy (an hallucinogenic amphetamine)

⇨ Tobacco

⇨ Anabolic steroids – used illegally to enhance strength and performance in sport

⇨ Amyl nitrite (poppers)

⇨ Cocaine

⇨ Crack cocaine.

Depressants

Depressants work by depressing the central nervous system. They can therefore induce a state of relaxation or sedation as well as reducing the intensity of pain and of emotions such as fear, anger or anxiety.

They can also have short-term effects of:

⇨ reducing intellectual ability and the ability to concentrate or retain information;

⇨ reducing motivation and energy;

⇨ reducing manual dexterity, e.g. the ability to operate machinery, drive, climb or swim.

Examples of depressants are:

⇨ opiates such as heroin/diamorphine (smack), morphine, pethidine and methadone;

⇨ benzodiazopines (tranquillisers such as Valium and Temazepam). These may be prescribed for short-term use to combat anxiety but they also have an illegal market;

⇨ cannabis (many street names such as hash, dope, weed, gear). Long-term use or high doses may lead to depression, increased anxiety, an inability to deal effectively with emotions, short-term memory loss, and insomnia;

⇨ alcohol.

Regular use of some of these drugs (e.g. opiates and benzodiazopines) may lead to physical dependency since withdrawal may result in unpleasant physical symptoms. There is also the danger of a serious, or even fatal, overdose due to the depressing of physical systems such as the heart and lungs.

Hallucinogens

These drugs enhance sensory perceptions – sight, sound, smell and touch.

UNIVERSITY OF CAMBRIDGE COUNSELLING SERVICE

On a pleasant 'good trip' a person may experience increased self- awareness and mystical or ecstatic feelings. On a 'bad trip' there may be unpleasant feelings of disorientation, panic, and/or paranoia. These may last several hours. People can also suffer 'flashbacks' where they relive experiences when tripping. This can be intensely disorientating and anxiety-provoking.

A bad trip is more likely in someone who is already anxious, depressed or unstable, or who takes the drug in an insecure environment. It may not be affected by previous experience of the drug or by dosage.

Hallucinogens include:

⇨ LSD

⇨ Hallucinogenic stimulants such as Ecstasy (see above)

⇨ Magic mushrooms

⇨ High-potency cannabis such as 'skunk'.

Possible side-effects and dangers of drugs

All drugs (medicinal as well as illegal) have the potential for unwanted, and often unexpected, effects. They are usually substance- and individual-specific.

The effects of a drug may vary according to the mental state of the person taking it. A strong mood-altering substance may trigger or exacerbate an underlying emotional instability.

Pleasurable effects followed by less pleasant after-effects may tempt someone into repeated use. Crack cocaine, for instance, can tempt someone into repetitive use very quickly because it gives a very strong but short-term 'burst' of euphoria followed by an equivalently intense coming-down which may include high anxiety as well as physical malaise. In addition, physiological tolerance may build up with some drugs so that more of the drug is needed to induce the desired effect.

Withdrawal from a drug in regular- or high-dosage use may lead to physical symptoms, i.e. there may be a physical dependency on the drug.

Drugs may interact with each other (including legal ones such as alcohol). Some mixtures may even prove life-threatening.

With any illicit drug, there is no quality control so there is a constant danger of variable strength and of adulteration with undesirable substances. Sources of cannabis may vary in potency by ten-fold, from 2% hash to 20% skunk. In the case of heroin, in particular, it is the unexpectedly pure drug which may kill someone who has insufficient tolerance.

Injecting drugs involves the risk of introducing infections directly into the bloodstream. Sharing of needles is particularly dangerous as it may lead to cross-infections (e.g. HIV and hepatitis).

Drugs taken during pregnancy may damage the foetus.

Heavy or regular drug use may be a symptom of a deeper malaise. People may turn to drugs in an attempt to avoid confronting problems or internal distress. This may work in the short term but can come to have severe financial, social, legal or physical consequences.

⇨ Information from the University of Cambridge Counselling Service: www.counselling.cam.ac.uk

get high

come down

Ketamine problems on the rise

Data from DrugScope's Street Drug Trends Survey 2011.

More drug services are seeing people coming forward for help with the drug ketamine, according to DrugScope's 2011 *Street Drug Trends Survey*, published in the November/December edition of the charity's *Druglink* magazine. The charity warns that many people who use, or are tempted to use, ketamine underestimate how harmful the drug can be.

The annual survey compiles and analyses feedback from 80 drug services, police forces, drug action teams and service user groups in 20 towns and cities across the UK. The survey provides an overview of patterns in the use and supply of drugs to give a snapshot of current UK street drug trends. The survey also compiles a national average price for different UK street drugs.

DrugScope's survey findings underline evidence of the growing presence of ketamine on the UK drug scene. Figures released by Avon and Somerset Police in July this year revealed that ketamine seizures had increased substantially at the Glastonbury Festival this year; later in the same month, the 2010/11 *British Crime Survey* (BCS) showed increases in reported use of the drug among those aged 16–24. The Home Office-commissioned research estimated that nearly 300,000 people had used ketamine at least once. This figure has risen from an estimated 140,000 users in 2007, after ketamine was added to the list of drugs surveyed following the drug's classification in 2006.

Of the 20 areas surveyed by DrugScope, three-quarters reported increases both in the general use of ketamine and in the numbers of people coming forward for help with psychological and physical problems associated with the drug. The average UK price for ketamine is approximately £21 a gram. It is currently controlled as a Class C drug under the Misuse of Drugs Act 1971.

Ketamine was originally developed in the 1960s as an anaesthetic, and proved valuable for battlefield surgery as the patient could be anaesthetised quickly. Hospital patients reported disturbing visions as they regained consciousness after surgery, however, meaning its medical use has since been more restricted, although it is used in veterinary medicine. Illicit supplies appear to come mainly from India, China and the Far East.

The risks relating to non-medical use of the drug are manifold. At sufficiently high doses of the drug, users may experience a 'K-hole'. This term refers to a subjective state which might include out-of-body experiences, confusion, temporary memory loss and vivid hallucinations. Use of the drug can become compulsive, particularly when injected. As the drug is an anaesthetic, some users can injure themselves without realising while under its influence; its hallucinatory properties can also increase the risk of injury through risk-taking behaviour. The drug depresses the respiratory system and use in conjunction with alcohol is particularly risky.

For long-term or dependent users, evidence is growing of the drug's harmful impact on the urinary tract, with some dependent users experiencing extreme bladder problems culminating in the need to wear a catheter for the rest of their lives.

> ## Many people who use, or are tempted to use, ketamine underestimate how harmful the drug can be

Martin Barnes, DrugScope's Chief Executive, said:

'Our survey findings underpin other evidence that use of ketamine appears to be on the rise, and that problems from using the drug are also now more apparent. People who use or are tempted to use ketamine need to know just how harmful this drug can be, and be able to access timely and professional help if required from their local drug services.

'In September, Kensington and Chelsea Hospital opened a new unit to treat people who have developed problems with so-called "club drugs" including ketamine; a similar unit was opened at the Maudsley Hospital in south London in 2009. However, the evidence presented to us by drug workers indicates that use of ketamine is not confined to those on the club or party scene – use is taking place across the community, from young people experimenting with drugs to those using heroin and crack.

'*Druglink* magazine first highlighted the harms associated with ketamine in 2000 – now that significant problems and evidence of increased use are beginning to emerge, it is very important that drug treatment and education services are sufficiently resourced to respond.'

16 November 2011

⇨ The above information is reprinted with kind permission from DrugScope. Visit www.drugscope.org.uk for more information.

DRUGSCOPE

'Safe ketamine': experts warn over trend for 'legal high' drug

Information from The Huffington Post.

By Kyrsty Hazell

A new 'legal high' drug is being mistakenly dubbed as the 'safe' version of ketamine and is becoming increasingly popular in the UK, a recent study has revealed.

According to widespread research by DrugScope, dangerous party drug ketamine has a legal doppelganger in the form of methoxetamine (MXE) or 'Mexxy', which mimics the effects of ketamine.

The *Druglink Street Drug Trends 2011* report, published in November by the drugs charity, discovered a growing trend of ketamine use in the UK, with MXE being marketed as the 'safer' version for drug-goers worried about the side-effects of ketamine.

The drug is sold as the 'bladder-friendly' substitute (referring to ketamine's most common side-effect – weakened bladder control) and is what insiders call a 'legal high' because the Misuse of Drugs Act doesn't control it.

The MXE drug manages to escape being classified as a Class A drug due to chemical structure differences but is still considered to be a 'controlled' substance, meaning it is illegal to possess, give away or sell.

Although it is illegal to sell the drug, dealers have found a legal loophole by selling it online, so long as they mark the items as 'not for human consumption'.

The casual labelling of this new drug is causing concern among health experts, who fear that its 'legal high' tag is misleading and dangerous.

'The new kid on the block seems to be methoxetamine,' Fiona Measham from the Independent Scientific Committee on Drugs told *The Independent*.

'It's so similar to the chemical structure of ketamine, there is no evidence to suggest that it doesn't carry the same risks, or that it is bladder-friendly.'

Martin Barnes, Chief Executive of DrugScope, told *The Huffington Post*: 'Users should not be fooled into thinking that because a drug appears to be legal that it is safe.

'Methoxetamine is one of a series of new drugs which have emerged onto the UK scene in the last couple of years; many have now been brought under the control of legislation, and others are currently under consideration by the authorities. So-called "legal highs" can be just as dangerous as any other drug.'

Although MXE use is a growing trend, ketamine is an increasing worry among drug charities and experts, after the research found it had expanded into 20 different areas demographically throughout the last year.

As a result of its popularity, a growing number of young, heavy users are suffering from old age-related conditions – such as impaired mental health and bladder damage.

Ketamine was recently linked to helping beat depression, with health experts reviewing whether it could be used to treat severe depression.

13 February 2012

⇨ This article first appeared in *The Huffington Post*. Visit www.huffingtonpost.co.uk for more information.

– IT'S SAFE, IT'S LEGAL, AND IT'S BLADDER FRIENDLY!

AND 'NOT FOR HUMAN CONSUMPTION'...?

Introduction to solvent and volatile substance abuse

Information from Re-Solv.

What is solvent and volatile substance abuse (VSA)?

VSA is when solvents and volatile substances are inhaled through the mouth and/or nose for the sole purpose of getting a 'high'.

Volatile substances are depressants which slow down the activity of the brain and central nervous system. This results in messages to and from the brain being slowed down, affecting the physical, mental and emotional responses. But unlike other drugs, volatile substances are unique in the fact that they can also be stimulants and cause hallucinations.

What are solvents and volatile substances?

Solvents and volatile substances are a range of products (many are everyday household items) that give off an intoxicating vapour.

There are two ingredients that are candidates for 'sniffing' – solvents and gases. They are described as volatile substances because they readily evaporate at room temperature and in doing so give off a 'sniffable' vapour.

Solvents are used to keep products dissolved until they are ready for use, e.g. to pour, spread or squirt and then to evaporate from the product quickly without a trace. This quick evaporation and volatility gives the intoxicating effect. If solvents were not used, the products would solidify in their containers.

As well as solvents being used to keep the products in a liquid state, they are also used to dissolve and liquefy materials once they have gone solid, i.e. nail varnish remover.

Gases are fuel gases, i.e. cigarette lighter refills or propellants.

Propellants are pressurised liquid gases used to propel the contents (deodorant, hairspray, paint, etc.) from the container. There are a number of these, but the main propellant used these days is butane.

There are more than 100 commercially available products that are now used to get a 'high'. In the home there may be over 30 'sniffable' products. Below are some of the products that can be 'sniffed':

⇨ Aerosols – deodorants, hairspray, paint spray, pain-relieving spray, air freshener, fly spray, etc.

⇨ Cigarette lighter refills.

⇨ Solvent-based adhesives.

⇨ Some typewriter correction fluids.

⇨ Nail varnish and nail varnish remover.

⇨ Dry-cleaning fluids.

⇨ Paint thinners and paint removers.

⇨ Fire extinguishers.

⇨ UHT cream – whipped cream cans.

⇨ Damp Start.

⇨ Dyes (for shoes).

⇨ Cleaning agents – degreasing materials, plaster remover, etc.

'Street' names

Listed below are some of the terms/names used to describe VSA:

⇨ Glue sniffing.

⇨ Solvent abuse/misuse.

⇨ Tooting – describes the misuse of gas and aerosols.

⇨ Sniffing.

⇨ Inhaling.

⇨ Buzzing gas.

Issues fast fact: VSA is highly dangerous. It kills more children aged ten to 15 than all illegal drugs put together.

⇨ The above information is reprinted with kind permission from Re-Solv. Visit www.re-solv.org for more.

© 2011 Re-Solv

RE-SOLV

Cannabis and schizophrenia

Information from Rethink Mental Illness.

We've undertaken a survey that has revealed that more than one in three (35%) of 25- to 34-year-olds agree or strongly agree with the statement 'experimenting with cannabis is a normal part of growing up'.

45% failed to link smoking cannabis over a sustained period of time to schizophrenia.

The poll also showed that those aged 18–24 have less liberal views on cannabis than the 25–34 age bracket, with just 24% agreeing with the same statement.

Cannabis facts

Cannabis can be a confusing subject – some people seem to use it without getting mental health problems. So what are the facts?

If you use it when young:

International studies have found that cannabis use doubles or triples the chances of developing psychosis if you smoke when you're under 18. The more you use, the greater the risk – in two studies, those who had used cannabis more than 50 times had six times the usual risk of developing schizophrenia. Most recently, a 2011 study commissioned by the German Government found that cannabis use doubles the rate of self-reported experience of psychotic symptoms in adolescents over a ten-year period.

If you use a lot of cannabis:

Smoking heavily at any age is also associated with mental health problems.

A 2008 study carried out by the Institute of Psychiatry (UK) found that people who had a psychotic episode were twice as likely to have used cannabis for longer, three times more likely to have used it every day and 18 times more likely to use skunk (a form of cannabis containing high levels of the active ingredient, THC).

If you already have a psychotic illness:

If you have a psychotic illness, cannabis use severely reduces your chances of getting better.

Why doesn't it affect everyone?

Not everyone will be affected by cannabis use – like peanuts, cannabis is very dangerous for some people, but not such a problem for others. Rethink Mental Illness is not claiming that cannabis causes psychosis in everyone who uses it. One study has suggested that this is because of people having different genes, but this has not yet been confirmed.

How many people are affected?

Two studies have estimated that 13% of schizophrenia could be averted if all cannabis use were prevented. One of these says that 50% of the most serious cases would be avoided.

What does Rethink Mental Illness want the Government to do?

We want a major public health campaign, like the campaign on smoking. The French Government spent over €3 million on a campaign about cannabis and mental health. And more research – no studies so far have been funded by the UK Government.

What about classification?

We think cannabis is a health issue; jailing people for cannabis use will not solve the problem. Money spent on policing cannabis should be spent on health education, services and research.

More than one in three (35%) of 25- to 34-year-olds agree or strongly agree with the statement 'experimenting with cannabis is a normal part of growing up'

Isn't cannabis a medicine?

Cannabis is a very complex substance, with over 60 active ingredients. It's a bit like crude oil – there are lots of different substances within it, all of which have different effects. One ingredient, THC Delta-9-tetrahydrocannabinol (THC), gets you 'high'. Another ingredient, Cannabidiol (CBD), relieves pain and prevents nausea.

Cannabis grown for cannabis-based medicines is designed to have very low THC. So it is a chemically different substance from the cannabis sold on the street, which is designed to have very high THC and small amounts of the other ingredients.

One other ingredient in cannabis (cannabidiol) has been trialled as a treatment for psychosis. Rethink Mental Illness supports this research and hopes it will produce a medicine that is effective for people with psychosis.

7 November 2011

⇨ The above information is reprinted with kind permission from Rethink Mental Illness. Visit www. rethink.org for further information.

RETHINK MENTAL ILLNESS

'Cannabis cure for brain cancer' headline is misleading

Information from Cancer Research UK.

By Kat Arney

Earlier this week the *Daily Mail* reported that a young US boy's brain tumour had been 'cured' after his father secretly gave him cannabis oil through his feeding tube.

The bold headline hides a more important truth: the boy was also receiving high-dose chemotherapy, and it is this – rather than the cannabis oil – that is likely to have treated his cancer.

Cannabis oil may well have helped to relieve some of the symptoms of the cancer, and treatment side-effects such as pain, nausea and appetite loss

Despite the headline, the story points out that the cannabis oil may well have helped to relieve some of the symptoms of the cancer, and treatment side-effects such as pain, nausea and appetite loss. But this isn't the impression that you get from reading the headline, which arguably implies that cannabis cured the boy's disease.

We felt it was important to emphasise this distinction. The role of cannabis and its derivatives in treating cancer is the subject of persistent Internet myth and rumour, and we're concerned that this headline may unduly fan these flames.

Cannabis and cancer – the state of play

One strand of the online rumours about cannabis and cancer is that there is some form of conspiracy to prevent research progressing into this area. This is not the case. In fact, we've previously written about how cannabinoids – the biologically active chemicals in cannabis – can slow the growth of tumours in lab tests.

But the fact remains that this work is still at an early stage. On top of this, there's no robust scientific evidence to show that cannabis or cannabis oil can successfully treat cancer. And it's possible that smoking cannabis can increase the risk of lung cancer.

At the moment, cannabis is illegal in the UK, although the medical use of cannabis and cannabis-derived chemicals is being investigated and debated.

The role of cannabis in treating cancer is the subject of persistent Internet myth and rumour

Cannabinoids do have the potential to be useful for cancer and other diseases, but this needs to be explored in rigorous and safe studies. And accurate headlines about cases such as this one would help too.

5 May 2011

⇨ Information from Cancer Research UK. Visit www.cancerresearchuk.org for further information.

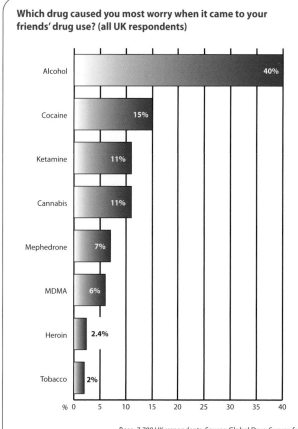

Which drug caused you most worry when it came to your friends' drug use? (all UK respondents)

Drug	Percentage
Alcohol	40%
Cocaine	15%
Ketamine	11%
Cannabis	11%
Mephedrone	7%
MDMA	6%
Heroin	2.4%
Tobacco	2%

Base: 7,700 UK respondents. Source: Global Drug Survey for Guardian/Mixmag, March 2012. © Guardian News & Media Ltd 2012

CANCER RESEARCH UK

Amy Winehouse's death prompts compulsory drug education in schools campaign

Information from the Press Association.

The death of Amy Winehouse has prompted a campaign to make drug education in schools compulsory.

The pop star 'might still be alive' if she had been educated about drugs, her father Mitch said on the eve of attending the launch of the campaign, supported by the Amy Winehouse Foundation.

An e-petition calling for effective drugs education to be part of the National Curriculum has been added to the Government's website.

The campaign wants approved drugs education and a separate drugs department, similar to that in France.

The petition, which will be launched in the House of Commons tonight, has been created by Maryon Stewart and Vicky Unwin, who both lost daughters as a result of drug use. Both are senior figures in the Angelus Foundation – which campaigns to highlight the dangers of 'legal highs', including alcohol. E-petitions can be considered for debate in Parliament if they get more than 100,000 signatures.

The petition says many legal highs and so-called club drugs are widely consumed by young people who regard them as safe because many are legal.

Winehouse, 61, said: 'We'll save hundreds of thousands of kids if we can do this.

'It's a disgrace that our children don't have drug education. It's preposterous.'

He added: 'We'll be saving future generations from a life of hell.'

Winehouse recently visited a rehabilitation clinic where a former addict spoke about the consequences of drugs with people currently battling the problem.

He believes that this method of educating youngsters can be effective and claimed that Amy, and the daughters of Stewart and Unwin, might still be alive if they had attended similar sessions.

He said: 'I wish that my daughter had had that kind of drug education when she was in her formative years.

'I think that had they had that education there's a good chance that all three of them would still be here today.'

Amy Winehouse was found dead in bed in her Camden flat, in July last year.

The singer battled with a drink and drugs problem during her life, prompting her father to set up the Amy Winehouse Foundation to help vulnerable youngsters in her memory.

Meanwhile, writing in *The Observer* yesterday, Unwin, whose daughter died after taking ketamine, said: 'On Wednesday March 2, 2011, our lives changed for ever.

'Our beloved 21-year-old daughter, Louise, who had everything to live for, drowned in her bath after taking an unintentional overdose of ketamine. She was not a regular drug user; she was a gregarious, popular, fun-loving girl who ... achieved more in her 21 years than most of us do in a lifetime.

'When Louise died, I knew immediately that she would want me to stop others from losing their lives in such a stupid and pointless way. I owed it to her memory and I knew that she would live on through my actions.'

Unwin said she took steps to raise awareness, posting messages on Facebook about her daughter's death, urging her friends to repost it on social networks and start a viral campaign.

Press coverage followed and as a result of one article she was contacted by Stewart, who set up the Angelus

Foundation after her 21-year-old daughter Hester died from a combination of a small amount of alcohol and a half-dose of GBL, a legal high.

The Foundation has campaigned on the issues surrounding legal highs.

In her *Observer* column, Unwin said: 'In the autumn we made a breath-taking discovery: that the Coalition Government, in its recent curriculum review, had abandoned Labour's bill to make the PSHE (personal, social and health education) curriculum compulsory, including drug education.

'This means that every school can decide how much curriculum time it wants to devote to drug education (for more than 60% of schools that means one hour or less a year), what the curriculum is (one recent study found that 70% of pupils couldn't recall any drug education in their secondary school), and who delivers it (it might be the PE teacher, the school nurse, and often it is a police officer or an ex-user who does an assembly).

'Most important, schools will not be measured on whether what they teach is successful or not. Research shows that drug education, poorly taught, can increase the use of drugs.

'So we decided to team up with the Amy Winehouse Foundation to launch a parents' petition to lobby government to make drug education part of the national curriculum. This campaign is being launched at the House of Commons on Monday.'

A Department for Education spokeswoman said: 'All pupils should have high-quality lessons to deal with the dangers of drug abuse. Schools have a legal responsibility to promote pupils' wellbeing – which should include setting out a clear drugs policy to prevent substance misuse.

'PSHE remains a compulsory part of the curriculum up to 16. Teachers know their pupils best and have the power to design their own lessons and decide what is taught. We are carrying out a detailed internal review to improve PSHE teaching and will set out next steps in due course.

'We published clear advice on drugs to schools last month setting out how they can address drug misuse – including giving accurate information through the FRANK campaign; working with charities and police to prevent it spreading, and providing pupils with clear information.'

5 March 2012

⇨ This article is reproduced with kind permission from the Press Association. Please visit www.pressassociation.com for more information.

© 2012 Press Association

Clever children more likely to take drugs

Information from the British Psychological Society.

Bright children who perform well in IQ tests may be more likely to indulge in illegal drug use later in life. This is the suggestion of new research published in the *Journal of Epidemiology and Community Health* – belonging to the Society for Social Medicine – which found this link is especially strong among women.

According to the study, men with high IQ scores at the age of five were found to be 50 per cent more likely to have taken drugs such as ecstasy and amphetamines by the time they reached 30.

In addition, the investigation revealed females who were clever as children were twice as likely as those who scored poorly to have tried such substances when they had grown up.

The authors noted previous research has suggested brainy youngsters may become easily bored or be teased by their peers, noting: 'Either of which could conceivably increase vulnerability to using drugs as an avoidant coping strategy.'

Men with high IQ scores at the age of five were found to be 50 per cent more likely to have taken drugs... by the time they reached 30

Dr Lucy Maddox, Child and Adolescent Clinical Psychologist from London, commented: 'This finding is interesting as it goes against what we might have expected to find.

'The finding is a correlation, so we can't say that higher IQ causes drug use, there may be other factors at play as well. Nonetheless, it does bring to mind the pressures that high-IQ, high-achieving children can be under and highlights the need to include all children in drug education.'

16 November 2011

⇨ The above information is reproduced with kind permission from the British Psychological Society. Visit www.bps.org.uk for further information.

© *The British Psychological Society*

The effects and impacts of drugs

Information from the Public Health Agency, Northern Ireland.

Social and community harm

This is determined by the type and method of drug misuse. Examples of harm to the community include:

⇨ theft;

⇨ cost of police, court system, prisons, probation orders, health and personal social services;

⇨ violence between drug users;

⇨ poor- or under-performance at school, college or work;

⇨ discarded needles, i.e. left in areas used by young people;

⇨ risk of spread of HIV infection, if injecting.

Where would you recommend your friends go for drugs-related information? (all UK respondents)

Friend or family member	33%
An independent drug info site	16%
GP	14%
Local drug service	16%
Drug user forum	9%
Telephone helpline	6%
Mixmag/Global Drug Survey	3%
Government website	3%

% 0   5   10   15   20   25   30   35

Base: 7,700 UK respondents. Source: Global Drug Survey for Guardian/Mixmag, March 2012. © Guardian News & Media Ltd 2012

Individual harm

Harm to the individual can take the form of ill health, social, personal or legal harm.

Ill health

Besides the actual nature and type of drug, the harm or risk to health can depend on:

⇨ exactly how much is taken;

⇨ the strength of the dose;

⇨ how often it is taken;

⇨ possible impurities in the drugs;

⇨ possible mixing of drugs together;

⇨ the person taking the drug.

Each individual will be affected in different ways by the same drug

Each individual will be affected in different ways by the same drug and the same amount of the drug. This is due to a number of factors, including:

⇨ make-up of individual (e.g. physiology; personality traits; physical and psychological health problems; weight; tolerance to drug; gender; family history; novice or regular user; method of use);

⇨ method of taking the drug (e.g. injecting; smoking; eating; sniffing; swallowing);

⇨ where the drug is taken (e.g. alone; at a party; at a club; outdoors; in the company of others).

The types of health-related harm that can be attributed to drug use include:

⇨ accidental overdosing – physical harm or death;

⇨ long-term excessive use – physical and psychological harm;

⇨ idiosyncratic reaction – physical and psychological harm;

⇨ novice use – physical and psychological harm.

The nature of the physical harm can range from increased blood pressure to collapse or death. Psychological harm can also range from feelings of anxiety through to acute psychotic behaviour and long-term mental illness.

Although a high proportion of those who take drugs do not come to any great harm, there is no guarantee. All drugs carry the risk of dependence.

Drug users can be viewed negatively and generally stigmatised by society

Social and personal harm

Drug users can be viewed negatively and generally stigmatised by society. This in turn can lead to feelings of low self-esteem and difficulties with various relationships. For example:

⇨ relationships with friends, family and employers may be harmed;

⇨ employment prospects can be damaged by having a criminal record or by poor or non-attendance at work or training scheme;

⇨ academic achievement and educational prospects may be harmed through poor- performance or by poor or non-attendance;

⇨ exclusion from school or college could affect educational prospects;

⇨ reputation may be hard to live down, leading to a person having to move.

Legal harm

Engaging in an illegal activity such as possessing or dealing in controlled drugs can leave a person with a criminal record, imprisonment or fines and may cause difficulty in obtaining work, visas or a passport.

⇨ Reproduced with kind permission from the Public Health Agency, Northern Ireland. For more information visit www.publichealth.hscni.net

Dependent drug users

Extract from the NTA report Drug Treatment in England: The Road to Recovery.

Estimates of the number of heroin and crack users in England fell from a peak of 332,000 in 2005/07 to 306,000 in 2009/10. More than half (172,139) are in community drug treatment and they make up 84% of the treatment population.

However, the number of adults newly entering treatment for heroin and crack use has fallen by 15% in two years. The number of 18- to 24-year-olds in this category has halved over five years. As the drug-dependent population ages, the over-40s have become the largest age group starting treatment. They tend to be entrenched users.

Estimates of the number of heroin and crack users in England fell from a peak of 332,000 in 2005/07 to 306,000 in 2009/10

Drug-related deaths in England peaked at 1,697 in 2001, then stabilised. There were 1,625 in 2010. This flat trend is reassuring as the injecting population is growing older and more vulnerable. Dependent users in treatment remain less likely to die from an overdose than those outside.

February 2012

⇨ The above information is reprinted with kind permission from the National Treatment Agency for Substance Misuse. Visit www.nta.nhs.uk for further information.

How to recognise drug abuse

Information from the Public Health Agency, Northern Ireland.

Physical signs

These can differ depending on the type of drug taken, e.g. stimulant or hallucinogenic. Below are some of the physical signs related to those illicit drugs known to be used in Northern Ireland. There is also information on heroin.

Stimulant drugs (amphetamines, butyl nitrite, cocaine) can cause:

⇨ increased pulse rate;

⇨ increased blood pressure;

⇨ agitation;

⇨ lack of coherent speech or talkativeness;

⇨ dilated pupils;

⇨ loss of appetite;

⇨ damage to nasal passages (tendency to sniff);

⇨ increased tendency to go to the toilet;

⇨ mouth ulcers;

⇨ fatigue after use.

Objects that may indicate drug use include:

⇨ small bottles, pill boxes;

⇨ twists of paper;

⇨ cigarette lighters;

⇨ spent matches;

⇨ aerosols, butane gas refills;

⇨ cigarette papers;

⇨ roaches (ends of rolled-up cigarettes);

⇨ needles;

⇨ the drugs themselves.

Ecstasy

Ecstasy is sometimes referred to as a hallucinogenic stimulant. Its effects will therefore include those listed for stimulants. In addition it can cause:

⇨ increased temperature;

⇨ possibly excessive sweating;

⇨ very dry mouth and throat;

⇨ hallucinations and heightened perceptions which may make users more tactile or dreamy;

⇨ jerky, uncoordinated movements;

⇨ repetitive movements – many users want to dance;

⇨ clenched jaws/grinding teeth;

⇨ uncontrolled jaw movements caused by muscle spasms;

⇨ occasional nausea when first used;

⇨ fatigue after use, possibly accompanied by some anxiety, depression and muscle pain;

⇨ weight loss.

It can be difficult to see signs in the experimental or casual drug user

Hallucinogens (LSD, magic mushrooms)

Effects can vary depending on the nature of the experience. They include:

⇨ relaxed behaviour;

⇨ agitated behaviour;

⇨ dilation of pupils;

⇨ uncoordinated movements.

Cannabis

Cannabis can have the effect of a depressant or mild hallucinogen, depending on the amount taken and situational factors. The short-term effects of taking cannabis include:

⇨ tendency to laugh easily;

⇨ becoming talkative;

⇨ more relaxed behaviour;

⇨ reddening of eyes;

⇨ dry mouth;

⇨ hunger.

If the drug is smoked, it produces a distinctive sweet smell.

Heroin

Heroin acts as a depressant. The short-term effects of taking heroin include:

- ⇨ slowing down of breathing and heart rate;
- ⇨ suppression of cough reflex;
- ⇨ increase in size of certain blood vessels;
- ⇨ itchy skin;
- ⇨ runny nose;
- ⇨ lowering of body temperature;
- ⇨ sweating.

Solvents

Solvents include glues, butane gas refills, aerosols, typewriting correcting fluids and thinners. Signs of solvent misuse include:

- ⇨ usual signs of intoxication;
- ⇨ possible odour on clothes and breath;
- ⇨ if using glue, redness around mouth and nose;
- ⇨ a cough;
- ⇨ possible stains on clothing depending on type of solvent used;
- ⇨ persistent coughing with a runny nose and eyes.

Behavioural signs

Drug use can often result in behavioural changes and you may need some prior knowledge of the person to make an accurate comparison. Such changes can be obvious or very subtle and may be due to another reason totally unconnected with drug use.

Behavioural signs can include:

- ⇨ efforts to hide drug use through lying, evasiveness and secretive behaviour;
- ⇨ sudden and regular changes of mood;
- ⇨ bouts of talkative, excitable and overactive behaviour;
- ⇨ unsatisfactory reasons for unexpected absences or broken promises;
- ⇨ more time spent away from home;
- ⇨ changes in friendships;
- ⇨ loss of appetite;
- ⇨ unusually tired;
- ⇨ unable to sleep at night;
- ⇨ changes in priorities, including less concern with school/college work, training scheme or paid employment, less care of personal appearance, non-attendance at usual recreational/leisure activities;

- ⇨ efforts to get money for drug use, ranging from saving dinner or allowance money, borrowing from friends and relatives and selling own possessions, stealing from friends and home and involvement in petty crime;
- ⇨ secretive telephone calls.

Other possible signs include:

- ⇨ being very knowledgeable about drugs and the local drug scene;
- ⇨ a defensive attitude towards drugs and drug-taking;
- ⇨ unusual outbreaks of temper;
- ⇨ absence from school, training scheme, college or work on days following attendance at nightclubs, parties, etc;
- ⇨ poor performance at school, training scheme, college or work.

These signs may often only become apparent in people who are using drugs on a regular basis. It can be difficult to see such signs in the experimental or casual drug user.

Ecstasy is sometimes referred to as a hallucinogenic stimulant

---

Possible signs of alcohol and drug misuse in the workplace

- ⇨ reduced work performance (characterised by, for example, confusion; lack of judgement; impaired memory; difficulty in concentrating on work; periods of high and low productivity);
- ⇨ absenteeism and time-keeping (e.g. poor time-keeping; increased absence; peculiar and increasingly improbable excuses for lateness and absence);
- ⇨ personality change (e.g. sudden mood changes; irritability and aggression; over-reaction to criticism; friction with colleagues);
- ⇨ physical signs (e.g. smelling of alcohol; loss of appetite; unkempt appearance; lack of hygiene);
- ⇨ feeding the addiction (e.g. attempting to borrow money from colleagues; dishonesty).

⇨ Reproduced with kind permission from the Public Health Agency, Northern Ireland. For more information visit www.publichealth.hscni.net

PUBLIC HEALTH AGENCY, NORTHERN IRELAND

Drug treatment in England: the road to recovery

The use of illegal drugs in England is declining; people who need help to overcome drug dependency are getting it quicker; and more are completing their treatment and recovering ...

The role of treatment

Drug workers – doctors, nurses, counsellors and others – help users overcome dependency.

They also help them to become active citizens, take responsibility for their children, earn their own living and keep a stable home. Drug users who are parents get extra support to look after their children.

While dependent users are in treatment they are less likely to use illegal drugs, to share needles and spread infections, or to steal and shoplift to fund their habit.

Research shows that crimes committed by users are halved when they are in treatment. It also indicates that most need at least three months in treatment to significantly reduce or stop their drug use.

It takes time for users to overcome addiction or manage it so they can lead normal lives. The average period in treatment is almost three years. Relapse is an ever-present risk.

Facts and figures

Drug treatment in England expanded to meet demand over the past decade and is now available to anyone who needs it.

The number of adults in treatment in 2010/11 was 204,473, more than double the number in 2001. the average wait has fallen from nine weeks in 2002 to five days, and 96% start treatment within three weeks.

Numbers peaked in 2008/09 but are now falling and likely to drop below 200,000 soon. since waiting times remain low, the decline probably reflects reduced demand rather than any shortfall in services.

Four out of five adults new to treatment either complete their programme or stay in long enough for them and society to feel the benefit.

Overall, the proportion staying in long enough to benefit is rising, the numbers leaving free from dependency are rising, and the numbers dropping out early are falling.

Successful completions more than doubled in five years to 27,969 in 2010/11. They went up by 150% compared to the figures for 2005/06, and the improvement is likely to be sustained this year.

Types of treatment

Four-fifths of adults in treatment are heroin users. The National Institute for Health and Clinical Excellence (NICE) recommends substitute prescribing as the most effective treatment for them, alongside talking therapies to change behaviour.

Some may benefit from detoxification or residential rehabilitation. A typical heroin addict can go in and out of treatment several times, experiencing repeated false dawns.

However, research published in the medical journal *The Lancet* found dramatic falls in drug use among newcomers to treatment, with more than one in three heroin users abstaining from the drug after six months.

Some argue that replacing an illegal drug with a legal one does not tackle addiction. However, this provides a platform for recovery, and it is better for everyone that a heroin addict gets a safe methadone prescription from a doctor than robs or steals to buy street heroin from a dealer.

Substitution options don't exist for crack addicts, or anyone dependent on cocaine or cannabis. Talking therapies are used, and the research in *The Lancet*

showed that half of crack addicts in such treatment were abstinent after six months.

Young people (under-18s)

The number of young people using drugs is falling. Around 22,000 under-18s were helped for substance misuse problems in 2010/11. Specialist services work with young people to prevent drug and alcohol use contributing to problems later in life, and to avoid addiction.

Nine out of ten of these young people have problems primarily with cannabis and/or alcohol. This is usually a symptom rather than a cause of their vulnerability, and reflects broader problems such as family breakdown, offending, truancy, anti-social behaviour and mental illness.

Addiction to Class A drugs is rare among young people, affecting fewer than one in 20 of those being helped. So interventions for under-18s differ from the treatment offered to dependent adults.

Treatment and recovery services

Central and local government spends about £800 million a year to provide a balanced range of treatment and recovery services. These are commissioned locally by 149 partnerships that represent councils, health authorities, the police, probation and other services. Local authorities will take on this role from April 2013 as part of a new duty to promote public health.

Meanwhile, local systems are reconfiguring to deliver recovery-orientated treatment, with more emphasis on enabling users to overcome dependency. As an incentive, 20% of the centrally allocated budget in 2012/13 will be based on success in ensuring users overcome dependency and do not return to treatment.

A mixture of NHS and voluntary sector organisations provide the services. Outcomes are monitored through the National Drug Treatment Monitoring System (NDTMS). The NTA's role in allocating funding, supporting local areas and measuring outcomes will be taken on by Public Health England from April 2013.

Getting better and getting on with life

A balanced system ensures that users get the treatment that is right for their individual needs.

But treatment alone can only go so far. The user must want recovery and be prepared for radical lifestyle change. Making and maintaining that change requires support from family, friends and mutual aid networks, education and employment opportunities, and community acceptance.

Every user in treatment has a personal care plan that assesses their needs and maps out the steps they will take. It also covers health, social functioning and criminal involvement.

Residential rehabilitation is suitable for some individuals at particular moments during their lives, but it is not the answer for every user. NICE recommends residential rehabilitation in complex cases for people who are ready to be drug-free, such as those who have been through detox but have not benefitted from community-based psychosocial treatments.

Key facts

⇨ The average wait for treatment in 2010/11 was five days, and 96% started within three weeks.

⇨ The numbers dropping out of treatment early are falling, the proportion staying in long enough to benefit is rising.

⇨ 28,000 adults left drug treatment free from dependency in 2010/11 – a 150% increase on the figure for 2005/06.

The wider benefits of treatment

Treatment aims to overcome dependency and reduce the harm drugs cause to users, their families and communities.

Chiefly, while heroin and crack addicts are in treatment they use fewer illegal drugs and commit less crime to fund the purchase of drugs from street dealers.

Less injecting, drug litter and blood-borne viruses also mean a reduced risk to public health. The UK now has one of the lowest rates of HIV among injecting drug users in the western world, and the incidence of hepatitis C among injectors in England is one of the lowest in Europe.

The National Audit Office has endorsed research findings that every £1 invested in drug treatment saves society £2.50 in the crime and health costs of drug addiction. The Home Office estimates that drug-related crime costs society £13.9 billion a year; NICE estimates the lifetime crime and health bill for every injecting drug user is £480,000. Additionally, users in treatment can cope better, can attend education and training, hold down jobs, and take care of their families.

Drug users are also more likely to complete their recovery if they have wider support to rebuild their lives, such as support with employment prospects and access to stable accommodation. Many rough sleepers are drug users, for example, but their drug use usually reduces significantly when their housing problems are solved. Mental illness is also linked to drug use, and users are more likely to recover when treatment and mental health services work together.

NATIONAL TREATMENT AGENCY FOR SUBSTANCE MISUSE

The results of treatment

The NDTMS database is one of the most comprehensive in the NHS and has collected robust data for six years.

The relapsing nature of addiction means we cannot assume all those who complete treatment will stay drug-free. However, we now have the ability to track the progress of everyone who went through the system across this six-year period.

⇨ Of the 255,556 adult drug users who entered treatment for the first time between 2005 and 2011, 28% (71,887) left free of dependency and have not returned since.

⇨ A further 33% (84,179) are still in treatment (although some may have left and subsequently returned).

⇨ The remaining 39% (99,490) left without completing their treatment but never returned either. Although some of these will have been in prison, and a few may have died, we can assume a significant proportion have overcome their dependency and recovered, despite their unplanned discharge from treatment. For some, walking away from treatment is about shaking off their identity as an addict and escaping the drug subculture.

The statistics reflect the often unpredictable nature of drug dependency and the ongoing cycles of relapse and remission. The most recent figures show that one in three individuals starting treatment for the first time in the past three years left free of dependency and have not returned.

The first step on the road to recovery

Increased investment expanded the availability of drug treatment and cut the time people waited for it. Having got record numbers of users into treatment quickly, the system is now responding to the recovery ambition of the 2010 Drug Strategy. Services are focused on moving people through treatment and getting them safely out the other end, with the aim of increasing the numbers recovering from dependency.

Drug workers are increasingly ambitious for users. Their goal is to help people recover from dependency and reintegrate themselves into society.

February 2012

⇨ The above information is reprinted with kind permission from the National Treatment Agency for Substance Misuse. Visit www.nta.nhs.uk for further information.

© *National Treatment Agency for Substance Misuse*

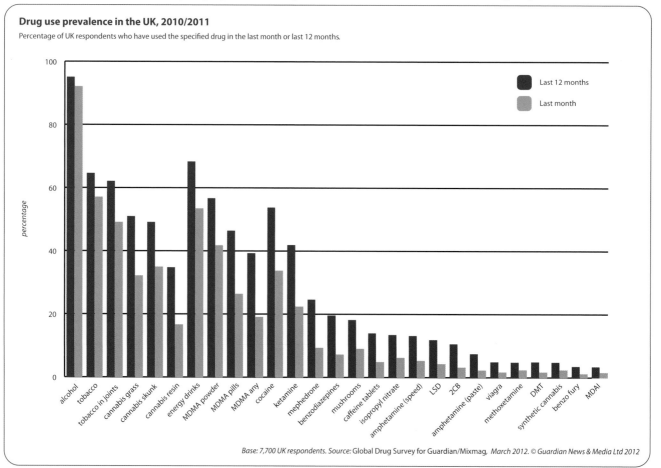

Drug use prevalence in the UK, 2010/2011

Percentage of UK respondents who have used the specified drug in the last month or last 12 months.

Base: 7,700 UK respondents. Source: Global Drug Survey for Guardian/Mixmag, March 2012. © Guardian News & Media Ltd 2012

'The story of what made me who I am'

Information from Wired In.

By Iain Donald

My name is Iain Donald. I was born and brought up in a small village on the outskirts of Aberdeen. What I can remember of my early years is always having what felt like a safe and secure family upbringing. Both my parents worked to provide this safe and secure setting for my sister and myself. And although we were never what you might call well-off, there was always food on the table and clothes on our backs.

While growing up I always seemed to be the master of underachievement and fell short, on many occasions, of what I now believe I was capable of. Although school was a really enjoyable experience for me, I treated it as a laugh and very rarely took it seriously. I was a bit of a daydreamer and joker, but these were still good times looking back.

My entire youth was spent enjoying school. And when I wasn't in school, I spent most weekends and holidays on my best friend's father's farm, a different life completely to what I would bear witness to later in my life.

After leaving school at the tender age of 16, I went straight into further education and studied agricultural engineering at college. Like much of my schoolwork, I never took this seriously either, and after only one year of the two-year course I left to work for my best friend's father on his farm. I was young and couldn't see the big picture. All I was looking for was the money. I've since came to regret this decision massively, as the last I heard, my best friend who completed the course was working for BP in Dubai.

If there was a single point where I can identify it beginning to go wrong, it would have been here. After this, my life consisted of various jobs. I got fed up of working, sometimes seven days a week, on the farm.

I moved on from being a farmer to a postman. Then my first long-term job was working for my father for eight years in his butcher's shop. This was unplanned, but at this time I'd started using ecstasy and other party drugs at the weekend and needed to fund this party lifestyle. I would have been 20 at the time, roughly. Looking back now, this was the beginning of a downward spiral for me due to my naive attitude towards drugs. If I am honest, I enjoyed this part of my life, although constant partying eventually took its toll.

The real destructive part of my life began shortly after this, with the progression from party drugs such as ecstasy and speed to harder drugs such as heroin, crack and cocaine. Initially, I convinced myself that, although I was smoking these drugs, I would never move on to injecting. However, this turned out to be another naive belief and it wasn't long before I began injecting one or a combination of these drugs.

In the beginning, I never anticipated this developing into the problem that it did, and my life began resembling a never-ending challenge to find enough funds to support my behaviour. At the time, I believed that my father, who I was still working for, was unaware of my trials and tribulations. I have since found out that he was aware that I was having difficulties, but was unaware of the extent to which these difficulties were controlling my actions.

Whilst still working for my father, my habit grew to such a level that the wages I was earning were insufficient to meet the increasing amount of drugs my head told me that my body needed. So much so that I began stealing money out of my father's shop. Indeed, stealing from the very hand that fed me. This process continued for many years.

During this period, I mostly lived with my parents in their home. My use of drugs took me on a voyage of discovery where I found out just how low I could go in order to satisfy my urge for drugs. I constantly borrowed money from my parents with various excuses for what I needed the money for. If this failed, I stole from them. Eventually, this led into crime.

I found myself breaking into pubs and shops and progressing onto street robbery. When I robbed someone, on the street in the village where I grew up and worked, of their money, this led to my arrest and imprisonment for one year. During my time in prison, I remained clean. This, however, was short-lived and almost immediately after I was liberated from prison my addictive nature took hold again and got worse than before.

My life continued with the age-old process of securing money and/or drugs and eventually led to me working for some major drug dealers, selling for them. This, of course, accelerated my habit even faster, as payment for selling for them was a personal supply of crack and heroin. During this time came a period of chaos which involved three overdoses that required hospitalisation, none of which was sufficient reason in my head to do anything about my problem.

The realisation finally came through when I found myself stealing from my sister's purse. Don't ask me why that was any different to the massive amount of money and peace of mind I stole from my parents. But it was. Shortly after this event, I moved into Phoenix Futures residential treatment in Glasgow.

After an 18-month+ period of clean time after leaving Phoenix Futures, during which I worked on a casual

basis for a heating engineer/plumber, which I enjoyed but which had no long-term prospects, I gradually felt myself stuck in a rut and discovered my life had become predictable and uninteresting. Before I realised the situation I was in, I had begun drinking at the weekends. This, however, did not stop at just a drink and after a very short time I began using cocaine along with the drink, again only at the weekends.

As I believed I was controlling it by only doing it at the weekends and working during the week, I didn't initially recognise this as being a problem. It didn't fully dawn on me, the situation that I'd got myself into, until the work I'd been doing dried up and I was left with nothing to do during the week. With money saved in the bank, my addiction took over and helped me spend that money in a matter of weeks.

It wasn't long until I was once again living from one dole cheque to the next. This continued for a while, during which time I started using heroin and crack, and this was only marginally controlled by how much money I had. It would have only been a matter of time before the urge to get more would have driven me to crime.

Although my addiction hadn't got quite as extreme as it was when I still lived in Aberdeen, the mental lows of relapsing after what I considered a reasonable amount of clean time were something I'd never experienced before. Even during the darkest parts of my life in Aberdeen.

I can't say for sure what made me realise my situation. I suppose I maybe had a moment of clarity, which got me thinking about my security. Even though I'd basically been living on bread and a jar of raspberry jam, I had been lucky by managing to keep hold of my flat, albeit with a habit which was ready to take off properly at any moment. I think it was around this time when I admitted defeat and got myself onto a methadone script.

Initially, I found it hard to stick to just my script and continued to use on top of it. This, however, did not last as I saw my methadone dose possibly spiralling out of control. When my methadone reached 55ml I decided enough was enough. My care manager suggested the Leaving the Blue and Green run by South East Alternatives. The only sticking point was it was preferred that you be 30ml or below at that time, to recognise the full potential of attending such a group.

By this time, I had caught a glimpse of something better than I'd had since moving to Glasgow in December 2006. An opportunity not only to become drug-free, but also the possibility of something more long-term being put in place to sustain my recovery. This gave me my initial goal to head for, getting to 30ml as soon as possible in order to start that group. Even though the group only ran once a week, on a Tuesday night, it kept me focused.

At the same time, I began playing football with some of the guys I'd go on to get to know better once I started the day project. The Tuesday night group and football gave me the drive and focus to believe that maybe things could be better. Having this drive and keeping my focus made my detox relatively easy.

Staying positive about my own ability to get off my methadone, and the possibilities that may arise once doing this, more than anything was the driving force behind my detox. Apart from a relatively short period of broken sleep, I felt no ill effects from the detox itself. I began to realise that it was, in fact, my own head that was trying to do a number on me by trying to make me believe it was too difficult to do. This was, however, something I refused to accept.

My opinion since this time has not altered. I believe the mind can, and does, control how an individual may feel in any given situation. And if you can control this part of the mind you give yourself a fighting chance of ridding yourself of the green death (methodone) for good.

My current prospects have never looked better, ever. And I only look forward. My past is nothing more than a painful memory, something which I will never forget, but certainly don't need to remind myself of.

⇨ Information from Wired In. Visit www.wiredin.org.uk for more.

Illegal drug use in the UK

Information from Politics.co.uk.

What are drugs?

Drugs include a broad range of substances, ranging from prescription medicines, to illegal street drugs such as cocaine and ecstasy, to readily available products such as tobacco and alcohol.

In public health and political terms, 'drugs' usually refers to recreational drugs, specifically those which are illegal under the Misuse of Drugs Act. Although technically a mind-altering substance, alcohol is not commonly included in the drugs debate, with binge drinking treated as a separate issue. Similarly, tobacco warrants its own debate.

Background

The UK Government has adopted a prohibitive stance towards recreational drugs, which is enforced through the Misuse of Drugs Act 1971. Prior to this Act, drugs policy in the UK was relatively liberal but was reformed under pressure from the US, who pushed for the global criminalisation of drugs.

This makes it an offence to possess drugs for personal use or with intent to supply, or to allow premises you occupy or manage to be used for drug-taking. It does not make it a specific offence to be under the influence of controlled substances.

The Act created the Advisory Council on the Misuse of Drugs (ACMD), which became responsible for distinguishing three separate classes of controlled substances, referred to as Class A, Class B and Class C drugs. This classification system both attempts to rank the harm caused by various drugs and set appropriate penalties for their use.

⇨ Class A: Ecstasy, LSD, heroin, cocaine, crack, magic mushrooms, amphetamines (if prepared for injection).

⇨ Class B: Amphetamines, cannabis, methylphenidate (Ritalin), pholcodine.

⇨ Class C: Tranquilisers, some painkillers, gamma hydroxybutyrate (GHB), ketamine.

When assessing the classification of new drugs, the ACMD hears evidence from law enforcement agencies, charities, professional bodies and scientific evidence. It classifies drugs using a risk assessment matrix, which covers nine types of term divided between physical harm, dependence and social harms.

Following an investigation by the ACMD, the Government brought a range of 'legal highs' under control of the Misuse of Drugs Act with effect from 23 December 2009. These included GBL (gamma-butyrolactone), BZP (benzylpiperazine) and 15 anabolic steroids, testosterone-like products often used by sports people, all of which are now designated Class C drugs. Synthetic cannabinoids – man-made chemicals sprayed on herbal smoking products – were also banned and are now designated Class B drugs.

In March 2010 the Government announced that mephedrone and its related compounds were to be banned on the recommendation of the ACMD and designated Class B drugs. The ACMD cited evidence that mephedrone consumption could cause hallucinations, blood circulation problems, anxiety, paranoia, fits and delusions.

Mephedrone and other cathinone derivatives became illegal with effect from 16 April 2010, the new legislation being by way of a 'generic definition' to make it difficult for suppliers to produce new versions of the substances. ACMD chair Professor Les Iversen described this generic legislation as a 'world first' for the cathinones.

POLITICS.CO.UK

As from November 2011, the Home Secretary has the power to invoke a temporary class drug order for new psychoactive substances that, following advice from the ACMD, are considered to be a cause for concern.

The Misuse of Drugs Act 1971, as amended by the Police Reform and Social Responsibility Act 2011, provides powers for enforcement agencies to deal with illicit manufacturers, suppliers and importers of temporary class drugs. Those found guilty of a temporary class drug offence could face up to 14 years' imprisonment and an unlimited fine.

The Sentencing Council for England and Wales published new sentencing guidelines for drug offences which came into force from February 2012.

Controversy

Drugs policy in the UK falls under the domain of the Home Office. This places it as a criminal matter and yet many argue drugs policy would be better overseen by the Department of Health. Similarly, the ABC drugs classification system has been criticised for combining physical and social harm caused with criminal penalties.

The UK adopts a policy of prohibition towards drugs. There is a body of thought that argues drugs policy should shift from abstinence education and government attempts to disrupt supply to harm-reduction policies. Small-scale versions of this approach tend to target existing addicts and focus on teaching people to avoid overdose, needle exchanges and opioid substitutes.

It has also been argued that criminalising all drugs by definition creates a criminal subculture to meet demand for recreational substances. This in turn has been linked to other forms of crime, including gang violence. However, calls to legalise all drugs are politically unpopular and the late Mo Mowlam is one of the few members of the political establishment to have made the case for legalising all hard drugs.

Drugs policy in the UK falls under the domain of the Home Office. This places it as a criminal matter and yet many argue drugs policy would be better overseen by the Department of Health

---

The ABC system for classifying drugs has come under intense criticism, both from within Parliament and from the scientific community.

Numerous sources have accused the ABC system of inconsistency, noting that the criminal penalties ascribed to various drugs do not always equate to the harm caused.

A study published in *The Lancet* in spring 2007 concluded that UK drugs policy was not fit for purpose. Looking at the harm caused by various narcotic substances, it found alcohol was the fifth most dangerous drug available, following heroin, cocaine, barbiturates and methadone,

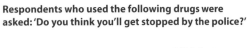

Respondents who used the following drugs were asked: 'Do you think you'll get stopped by the police?'

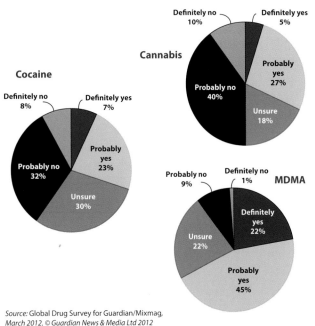

Cannabis
- Definitely no 10%
- Definitely yes 5%
- Probably yes 27%
- Unsure 18%
- Probably no 40%

Cocaine
- Definitely no 8%
- Definitely yes 7%
- Probably yes 23%
- Unsure 30%
- Probably no 32%

MDMA
- Probably no 9%
- Definitely no 1%
- Definitely yes 22%
- Unsure 22%
- Probably yes 45%

Source: Global Drug Survey for Guardian/Mixmag, March 2012. © Guardian News & Media Ltd 2012

Drugs and the law

Class	Drug	Possession	Production/supply
A	Cocaine, crack, ecstasy, heroin, LSD, magic mushrooms, methadone, methamphetamine, peyote, PMA, 2CB	Up to seven years in prison, a fine, or both	Up to life in prison, a fine, or both
B	Amphetamine, cannabis, synthetic cannabinoids (Spice), cathinones (mephedrone), narphyrone	Up to five years in prison, a fine, or both	Up to 14 years in prison, a fine, or both
C	Ketamine, piperazines (BZP), GHB, GBL, tranquilisers, anabolic steroids	Up to two years in prison, a fine, or both	Up to 14 years in prison, a fine, or both

Drugs are classified into three categories, with Class A substance using and dealing having the heaviest penalties attached. Adults and young people are considered differently by the criminal justice system, with different penalties applying. However, any criminal record can make it difficult for you to get a job, get into college, or get a visa if you want to travel abroad.

Source: Drugs and the Law: www.thinkdrinkdrugs.co.uk
© 2010, Health Promotion Substance Misuse Team Brighton & Hove

POLITICS.CO.UK

yet it is not included in the ABC system. Tobacco emerged as the ninth most dangerous drug, ahead of cannabis and the Class A drugs ecstasy and LSD.

The decision to include or reclassify a drug in the ABC system is invariably met with further controversy. Rising expectation in 2006 that crystal meth was set to surge in popularity in the UK led many to argue it should be reclassified as a Class A drug, underscoring the harm caused by the amphetamine. However, concerns were raised that the resultant publicity from reclassifying the drug would draw attention to its effects and inadvertently increase its use. Nevertheless, in January 2007, crystal meth was reclassified as a Class A drug.

The reclassification of cannabis has provoked similar controversy. In 2004 it was revised downwards from a Class B to a Class C drug after it was argued this would give police more time to concentrate on 'hard' drug users. In practice this meant it was unlikely an adult caught in possession of cannabis would be arrested and charged. Instead they would likely receive a warning and have the drug confiscated, unless certain conditions applied.

A selection of anti-drug campaigners, scientists and MPs argued the reclassification of cannabis was inappropriate and ignored the evidence that stronger strains of 'skunk' cause more harm than the cannabis available during the 1960s and 1970s. In summer 2007 Gordon Brown indicated he was prepared to reclassify cannabis as a Class B drug and in January 2009, the Government reclassified cannabis as a Class B drug. The decision was part of the 2008 drug strategy *Drugs: protecting families and communities.*

The decision to ban mephedrone in 2010 was also controversial, with one member of the ACMD resigning over the issue. In his resignation letter, Eric Carlin said: 'We had little or no discussion about how our recommendation to classify this drug would be likely to impact on young people's behaviour. Our decision was unduly based on media and political pressure.'

Mephedrone, also known as MCAT, meow and bubbles, was said to be increasingly popular amongst recreational drug users and suggestions that the drug had been involved in over 20 deaths attracted considerable media attention. Several serious side-effects had been reported, but as the charity DrugScope pointed out, there was 'no significant clinical literature' available on the effects of mephedrone and the other cathinone derivatives.

An editorial in *The Lancet* suggested the ACMD did not have sufficient evidence to judge the harms caused by this drug class and warned: 'Making the drug illegal will also deter crucial research on this drug and other drug-related behaviour, and it will be far more difficult for people with problems to get help.'

Sentencing for drug offences also attracts controversy. DrugScope expressed particular concern about seemingly high sentencing tariffs for women coerced or intimidated into trafficking drugs ('drug mules') and welcomed the new sentencing guidelines published in 2012 by the Sentencing Council for England and Wales. The charity felt this particular concern had been 'partly addressed' by the new guidelines, but remained concerned that the sentences for 'drug mules' may still be 'lengthy'.

A study published in The Lancet in spring 2007 concluded UK drugs policy was not fit for purpose

---

DrugScope also welcomed the Council's decision that community orders should be considered as a realistic alternative to prison for drug-dependent individuals, and questioned once again whether using the criminal justice system to respond to offences of drug possession was 'the most effective way to reduce drug-related harms both to individuals and the wider community'.

Quotes

'The Sentencing Council's guideline brings sentencing guidance together for the first time to help ensure consistent and proportionate sentencing and provide effective guidance for sentencers and clear information for victims, witnesses and the public on how drug offenders are sentenced.'

Sentencing Council. Drug Offences: Definitive Guideline *– February 2012*

'It's clear that the Sentencing Council has carried out a careful and considered consultation on sentencing for drug offences. We're pleased that the Council has taken on board much of the evidence submitted by organisations such as DrugScope.

'As a result of these changes to the guidelines, we are hopeful that more judges will feel able to refer people who are dependent on drugs for treatment as part of a sentence for a drug-related offence. Good quality treatment is instrumental to breaking the cycle of drugs and crime which blight the lives of many individuals and communities.'

Martin Barnes, Chief Executive of DrugScope – 2012

⇨ The above information is reprinted with kind permission from Politics.co.uk. Visit www.politics.co.uk for further information.

© *SquareDigitalMedia Ltd*

POLITICS.CO.UK

Drug policy: legislation, strategies and economic analysis

Extract from the Department of Health report United Kingdom Drug Situation 2011 Edition, UK Focal Point On Drugs.

Introduction

The United Kingdom consists of England, Wales, Scotland and Northern Ireland. England accounts for 84% of the UK population. A number of powers have been devolved from the United Kingdom Parliament to Wales, Scotland and Northern Ireland, but each has different levels of devolved responsibilities.

The Misuse of Drugs Act 1971 is the principal legislation in the United Kingdom with respect to the control and supply of drugs that are considered dangerous or otherwise harmful when misused. This Act divides such drugs into three Classes (A, B and C) to broadly reflect their relative harms and sets maximum criminal penalties for possession, supply and production in relation to each class. Drugs in Class A include cocaine, ecstasy, LSD, magic mushrooms, heroin, methadone, methylamphetamine and injectable amphetamine. Class B drugs include amphetamine, barbiturates, cannabis and, since April 2010, cathinones including mephedrone. Class C drugs include anabolic steroids, tranquillisers, ketamine, and since December 2009, BZP and GBL. The Drugs Act 2005 amended sections of The Misuse of Drugs Act 1971 and The Police and Criminal Evidence Act 1984, strengthening police powers in relation to the supply of drugs. The Police Reform and Social Responsibility Act 2011 added provisions for 12-month temporary class drug orders enabling enforcement activity against the traffickers and suppliers of new psychoactive substances.

The Misuse of Drugs Act 1971 is the principal legislation in the United Kingdom with respect to the control and supply of drugs

The United Kingdom Government is responsible for setting the overall strategy and for its delivery in the devolved administrations only in matters where it has reserved power. A new drug strategy was launched in December 2010 replacing that of the previous Government, which was published in 2008. Within the strategy, policies concerning health, education, housing and social care are confined to England; those for policing and the criminal justice system cover England and Wales.

The Scottish Government and Welsh Government's national drug strategies were published in 2008, the latter combining drugs, alcohol and addiction to prescription drugs and over-the-counter medicines. All three strategies aim to make further progress on reducing harm and each focuses on recovery. The Scottish and Welsh strategy documents are also accompanied by an action or implementation plan, providing a detailed set of objectives; actions and responsibilities; expected outcomes, and a corresponding time scale. Each plan reflects the devolution of responsibilities to the national government.

Northern Ireland's strategy for reducing the harm related to alcohol and drug misuse, the New Strategic Direction for Alcohol and Drugs (NSD), was launched in 2006. The NSD contains actions and outcomes, at both the regional and local level, to achieve its overarching aims. A review of the NSD was conducted in 2010, and a revised document was issued for public consultation in March 2011. It is anticipated that the revised document, entitled the *New Strategic Direction for Alcohol and Drugs Phase 2 – 2011-2016* will be published later in 2011.

After the change in government in 2010, performance targets in England were abolished. However, elsewhere in the UK, drug strategies are underpinned by performance management frameworks, including Public Service Agreements (PSAs) and associated sets of performance indicators, which progress is measured against.

Labelled public expenditure on drugs is about €1.3 billion (£1.1 billion) per annum. The economic and social costs of Class A drug use in England and Wales combined are estimated to have been around €22.2 billion (£15.4 billion) in 2003/04. Using a similar methodology, it is estimated that the economic and social costs of illicit drug use in Scotland was €5.1 billion (£3.5 billion) in 2006.

Legal framework

Drugs controlled under the Misuse of Drugs Act 1971 are listed as Class A, B or C under Schedule 2 of the Act. The ABC classification system of drugs is based on a broad assessment of the comparative health and social harms of controlled drugs and their misuse. It also provides the criminal justice system with a legal framework within which maximum criminal penalties are determined.

Classification of drugs

This section represents the situation as at 30 September 2011.

Temporary class drug orders

The introduction of a new power extending the remit of the Misuse of Drugs Act 1971 to control new psychoactive substances which raise sufficient concern to justify a faster legislative response forms part of the Government's Drug Strategy published in December 2010. The Police Reform and Social Responsibility Act 2011 was given Royal Assent on 15 September 2011. Section 151 and Schedule 17 make provision for the power to invoke a temporary class drug order. It is expected that the power will be available to the Secretary of State by the end of 2011. The importation, exportation, production and supply of a temporary class drug will be prohibited, although simple possession will not be unlawful. Under Schedule 17 of the 2011 Act, the Secretary of State must consult the Advisory Council on the Misuse of Drugs (ACMD) before invoking a temporary class drug order. The ACMD is also able, of its own volition, to recommend to the Secretary of State that a substance be subject to a temporary class drug order. Temporary class drug orders will be in force for up to 12 months, subject to parliamentary approval being given within 40 days of the order being laid under the 'made affirmative' resolution procedure, eight or less if revoked or the temporary class drug is brought under permanent control within this timeframe. This will allow the ACMD to collate and make a full assessment of harm to provide full advice to the Government on control under the 1971 Act.

A new joint Working Protocol agreed between the Home Secretary and the ACMD will also be placed in the Houses of Parliament Libraries – a draft of this document is currently available in Parliament. The Working Protocol is a shared document which sets out how the Government and ACMD interact, and the framework within which the ACMD is to provide advice concerning temporary class drug orders.

Tapentadol and amineptine

The ACMD provided advice to the Government, which was accepted, on the control and classification of tapentadol and amineptine under the Misuse of Drugs Act 1971. These were approved by Parliament so tapentadol and amineptine became controlled Class A and C drugs, respectively, on 18 March 2011.

Phenazepam

In July 2011, the Government also accepted the ACMD's advice to add phenazepam to the list of benzodiazepines, which are controlled Class C drugs under the 1971 Act. Pending control, the Home Office imposed a ban on the importation of phenazepam, which is being sold as a 'legal high' on the Internet. The ACMD's advice summarised the health harms of phenazepam and highlighted concerns that, as a potent member of the benzodiazepine family (with a potency five times that of diazepam), the risk of overdose is high.

Desoxypipradrol and related compounds

In September 2011, the ACMD provided further advice to Government on desoxypipradrol (2-DPMP), the importation of which was banned in November 2010 following initial advice. The ACMD's advice also identified structurally related compounds, such as diphenylprolinol (diphenyl-2-pyrrolidinylmethanol or D2PM) and 2-diphenylmethylpyrrolidine, and formulated a generic definition to capture them along with 2-DPMP under the 1971 Act. Ministers accepted the ACMD's assessment of evidence on 2-DPMP and structurally related compounds, identified in some 'legal high'-branded samples of 'Ivory Wave' in 2010, including its recommendation to control them as Class B drugs under the 1971 Act on the basis of harm they pose.

The Government is expected to seek parliamentary approval to ban phenazepam as a Class C drug and 2-DPMP and related compounds by generic definition as Class B drugs under the Misuse of Drugs Act 1971 by the end of 2011.

Advisory Council on the Misuse of Drugs (ACMD)

Constitution of the ACMD

The Police Reform and Social Responsibility Act 2011 amended Schedule 1 of the Misuse of Drugs Act 1971 regarding the constitution of the ACMD. Section 152 removes the requirement to have at least one member with expertise in each of six areas of scientific practice: medicine; dentistry; veterinary medicine; pharmacy; the pharmaceutical industry, and chemistry. It also removes the requirement to have members who have experience of social problems connected with drug misuse. These stipulations are intended to allow for greater flexibility in the ACMD's membership to respond to changes in the drugs landscape, particularly in dealing with new psychoactive substances. The list of statutory areas of members' expertise has been replaced by a more detailed, non-statutory list of likely relevant areas of expertise from which the ACMD's membership should be drawn. This list is published in the Working Protocol agreed between the ACMD and the Government and will be kept under review, as a joint exercise, by both parties.

Review of the ACMD

Findings from a review of the ACMD by Sir David Omand were published in 2010. The review aimed to discover whether the ACMD is able to discharge the function it was set up to deliver and whether it represents continuing

DEPARTMENT OF HEALTH

value for money. It was concluded that the ACMD has been effective within the resources given and represents excellent value for money. The review recommended that the ACMD should continue to provide advice on its own initiative, in addition to meeting the requirements of the Government, and that Ministers should respond to advice within six weeks. It was also recommended that the ACMD should agree a three-year rolling programme annually and that the Government should provide the ACMD with a co-ordinated set of priorities. The Government and ACMD have embedded a number of Sir Omand's recommendations in the Working Protocol.

Proposed revisions to legal framework

Drug driving law

The House of Commons Transport Committee (2010) published a report on its inquiry into drink and drug driving law. Announced in July 2010, the inquiry focused on the more high-profile and controversial recommendations from the North Review. The Committee recommended that the Government develop a five-year strategy for tackling drug driving and welcomed the Government's commitment to install drug screening devices in every police station by 2012. It also recommended the adoption of a 'zero tolerance' approach to illegal drugs known to impair driving.

The Government published its response to the reports of the North Review and House of Commons Transport Committee (HM Government 2011). It proposes implementing recommendations to amend the Road Traffic Act 1988 to allow nurses to assess whether a drug driving suspect 'has a condition which might be due to a drug' in addition to Forensic Physicians who currently undertake that role. Other recommendations to be implemented include the provision of training to health professionals involved in assessing those suspected of drug driving and type approval of preliminary drug screening devices to police stations within two years. A specification for a station-based device has been approved and manufacturers have submitted devices for type approval. The Government intends to continue exploring the issues around the creation of a new offence and to research the possibility of either introducing threshold limits for drugs or adopting a zero-tolerance approach.

Provision of foil

A report into the use of foil as a harm-reduction measure for heroin users explored the legal status of providing foil to users. After reviewing international evidence, the ACMD report concludes that there is no evidence of any harmful effect from the provision of foil. Given the potential harm reduction benefits, the ACMD recommends that foil be exempt from Section 9A of the Misuse of Drugs Act 1971, which makes it an offence to supply any article for the purpose of administering a controlled drug illegally.

Anabolic steroids

The ACMD has provided advice to the Government recommending that the importation of anabolic steroids be restricted to personal custody and the term 'medicinal product' be removed from the Misuse of Drugs Regulations 2001. The Government has accepted the ACMD's advice. The Government intends to implement the ACMD's recommendations by December 2011.

'Sativex'

The ACMD also reviewed its advice to the Government on the scheduling of the medicinal product 'Sativex' oromucosal spray under the Misuse of Drugs Regulations 2001, following the grant by the Medicines and Healthcare products Regulatory Agency (MHRA) of its Marketing Authorisation in June 2010.

Forthcoming advice

The ACMD will publish its thematic advice to the Government on tackling new psychoactive substances and the so called 'legal high' market in October 2011. It is also working on a review of cocaine and advice on polysubstance use, and its working group on treatment is now on the Recovery Standing Committee to enable the delivery of the recovery agenda in the Government's Drug Strategy. Its review of khat, another work priority agreed between the Home Secretary and the ACMD, will begin in autumn 2011.

Commentary and research

Drug control legislation and legal highs

A joint report published by the United Kingdom Drug Policy Commission (UKDPC) and Demos explored whether current drug control legislation is appropriate for today's drug market, specifically focusing on the issue of 'legal highs'. The authors view drug policy as a 'wicked issue' where there is no right or wrong and no simple solution. By using a framework that seeks consensus and avoids polarising the debate, the authors believe progress in drug policy can be made. The report states that there is a 'fundamental and growing bias in the political and regulatory system towards prohibition as a default option'. This, the authors claim, may actually increase harms and have large financial implications. The report provides a number of recommendations within three broad principles:

⇨ focus on achieving outcomes on which there is a consensus;

⇨ ensure a more balanced decision-making process and debate, including conducting more rigorous

research on the impacts of drug control and giving greater consideration of the benefits as well as harms of drugs; and

⇨ consider other regulatory options for control, including the use of consumer protection legislation, and consider an integrated framework for controlling harmful substances (including alcohol and tobacco), possibly through a Harmful Substances Control Act.

National action plan, strategy, evaluation and co-ordination

Advisory Council on the Misuse of Drugs

The Home Secretary wrote to the ACMD in February 2011 setting out her priorities for the ACMD during 2011/12. The letter asks for the issue of 'legal highs' to be prioritised in the ACMD's work programme and for a review of cocaine harms to begin immediately, with a review of khat undertaken at the next available opportunity. Other strands of work for the ACMD include a polysubstance working group and an inquiry into treatment effectiveness to drive the delivery of the 'recovery' focus in the Government's Drug Strategy.

Drug Strategy 2010

A new drug strategy, *Reducing Demand, Restricting Supply, Building Recovery*, was published by the Coalition Government in December 2010. The strategy emphasises recovery and supporting people to become drug-free. It also aims to restrict supply by cracking down on Internet sales, reducing supply in prisons, developing an approach to stop criminals profiting from the trade in cutting agents and strengthening international partnerships. Some of the key initiatives of the strategy are to:

⇨ introduce a system of temporary bans on new psychoactive substances;

⇨ pilot wing-based, abstinence-focused drug recovery services in prisons;

⇨ pilot Payment by Results (PbR) schemes for drug recovery; and

⇨ develop and evaluate alternative forms of treatment-based accommodation for offenders.

For the first time, the strategy includes dependence on all drugs, including prescription and over-the-counter drugs and, where appropriate, severe alcohol dependency.

This strategy is for the period 2010/11 to 2014/15. The Government is putting in place the infrastructure and mechanisms that will enable delivery on its commitments. This is supported by strong governance arrangements to monitor, drive implementation, and review the outcomes of the strategy led through an inter-ministerial group of cross-government ministers. In

addition to this, the Government will conduct an Annual Review of the progress and outcomes made for each of the four years of the strategy.

The Government is working with a newly-formed Recovery Partnership, bringing together the Substance Misuse Skills Consortium, the Recovery Group UK and DrugScope. The aim of this is to facilitate change within the sector away from a treatment to a recovery focus.

A summary of the responses to the consultation on the drug strategy, carried out in 2010 (see *2010 UK Focal Point Report*) was published alongside the strategy document.

27 October 2011

⇨ The above information is reprinted with kind permission from the Department of Health. Visit www.dh.gov.uk for further information.

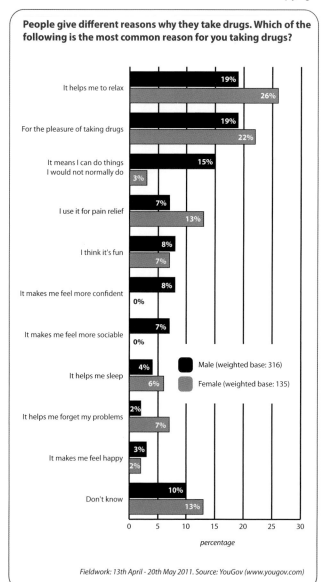

People give different reasons why they take drugs. Which of the following is the most common reason for you taking drugs?

Reason	Male	Female
It helps me to relax	19%	26%
For the pleasure of taking drugs	19%	22%
It means I can do things I would not normally do	15%	3%
I use it for pain relief	7%	13%
I think it's fun	8%	7%
It makes me feel more confident	8%	0%
It makes me feel more sociable	7%	0%
It helps me sleep	4%	6%
It helps me forget my problems	2%	7%
It makes me feel happy	3%	2%
Don't know	10%	13%

Male (weighted base: 316)
Female (weighted base: 135)

percentage

Fieldwork: 13th April - 20th May 2011. Source: YouGov (www.yougov.com)

Sentencing guideline for drug offences comes into force

The new definitive guideline on drug offences will be used in all courts in England and Wales from 27 February 2012.

The Sentencing Council's guideline brings sentencing guidance together for the first time to help ensure consistent and proportionate sentencing and provide effective guidance for sentencers and clear information for victims, witnesses and the public on how drug offenders are sentenced.

The Sentencing Council has also produced several sentencing scenarios to familiarise sentencers with the guideline's approach and process.

Possession of a controlled drug with intent to supply it to another (Misuse of Drugs Act 1971 section 5[3])

Louise is an 18-year-old pupil at a college. She is arrested in the school grounds by police and is charged with possession with intent to supply cannabis. She is found with 24 plastic bags in her rucksack, each containing 5g of cannabis, in total 120g of cannabis.

When the police interview Louise she says that the cannabis is for her friends. She fully co-operates with police, stating that her uncle had supplied her with the drugs for her to sell on to her friends.

Louise was told to charge £15 per bag which was to be given to her uncle. Louise explained that she is very scared of her uncle; he has been physically violent towards her and her sister in the past and Louise was worried what might happen if she did not do what her uncle told her to do.

Police records show they have been called to the home address on a number of occasions. Louise says she knows it was wrong and she did it purely through fear and had no thought to making any financial gain from the drugs. It is clear that Louise, whilst an adult, is naive for her age. Louise has since been expelled from college. Louise has no previous convictions and pleads guilty at the earliest opportunity.

Step one

The guideline for possession of a controlled drug (Class B) with intent to supply it to another applies. In this case it is likely that the court will find the defendant to be in a lesser role, as she was engaged through pressure and intimidation by her uncle, who exploited her naivety.

In terms of harm, as the offence involves selling directly to users ('street dealing'), the harm category is category 3, irrespective of the amount of drugs involved.

Lesser role/category 3 has a range of a low-level community order to 26 weeks' custody. The starting point is a high-level community order.

Step two

The court will want to consider Louise's lack of previous convictions and assess whether her age indicates a lack of maturity.

Ketamine is a Class C drug so the offence category is category 3

It will be for the court to decide the extent of any adjustment, but given that Louise has no previous convictions and the presence of the personal mitigation, the court would likely consider that, on balance, the starting point of a high community order should remain the appropriate sentence.

Step three

There are no other factors indicating a reduction in sentence.

Step four

There is a guilty plea at the earliest opportunity, which will lead to a reduction in the punitive elements of the community order.

The likely sentence is a medium community order for 12 months with the following requirements:

1 Supervision order (rehabilitative element).

2 Unpaid work in the range of 100 to 200 hours (1/3 reduction from recommended 150 to 300 hours to reflect guilty plea).

Step five

The totality principle is not applicable here as it is a single offence.

Step six

Destruction of the drugs is ordered.

SENTENCING COUNCIL

Step seven

The court should set out the reasons for its sentence.

Step eight

The defendant has been on unconditional bail so no adjustment for remand time is required.

Possession of a controlled drug with intent to supply it to another (Misuse of Drugs Act 1971 section 5[3])

Damien, 23, is observed by police officers acting suspiciously in an inner city estate. The police officers see him remove a package from his pocket which he puts into his rucksack. Damien sees the police officers and runs off. The officers catch up with him and, on searching Damien's rucksack, find the package, which contains 20 wraps of cannabis (80g in total). There is also a quantity of cash and some incriminating text messages on his mobile phone. Damien pleads guilty at an early stage to one count of possession with intent to supply. Damien has previous convictions of possession with intent to supply, a number of those convictions involved Class A drugs.

Step one

The guideline for possession of a controlled drug (Class B) with intent to supply it to another applies.

In this case it is likely that the court will find the defendant to be in a significant role since he is motivated by financial advantage.

In terms of harm, as the offence involves selling directly to users ('street dealing'), the harm category is category 3, irrespective of the amount of drugs involved.

Significant role/category 3 has a range of 26 weeks' to three years' custody. The starting point is one year's custody.

Step two

Damien's previous convictions are a statutory aggravating factor. There are no mitigating factors. It will be for the court to decide the extent of any adjustment but, given Damien's previous convictions of possession with intent to supply, the court would likely consider that a sentence of two years' custody is appropriate.

Step three

There are no other factors indicating a reduction in sentence.

Step four

There is a guilty plea at an early stage which will lead to a reduction in the sentence. The likely sentence is 16 months' custody.

Step five

The totality principle is not applicable here as it is a single offence.

Step six

Destruction of the drugs is ordered.

Step seven

The court should set out the reasons for its sentence.

Step eight

The defendant has been on unconditional bail so no adjustment for remand time is required.

Possession of a controlled drug (Misuse of Drugs Act 1971 section 5[2])

Rachel, 28, is found by a police officer slumped on the pavement at a bus station in the early hours. It is clear that Rachel is unconscious and the officer is unable to rouse her. The officer immediately calls an ambulance and on a quick inspection of her purse finds a small bag containing white powder residue which is later found to be ketamine. The paramedics arrive and Rachel is taken to hospital. Rachel is later charged with possession of ketamine.

Rachel has one previous conviction for possession of ketamine from six months ago when she received a £200 fine and two cautions for the same offence in the past 18 months. Rachel freely admits she is a recreational user of ketamine, using it occasionally when she goes out clubbing. In the police interview she is clearly shaken by the experience and is remorseful, fully understanding how vulnerable she made herself that night. She pleads guilty at the earliest opportunity.

Step one

The guideline for possession of a controlled drug applies.

Ketamine is a Class C drug so the offence category is category 3.

Category 3 has a range of a discharge to a medium level community order and a starting point of a band A fine.

Step two

Rachel's previous conviction is a statutory aggravating factor. Rachel has a previous conviction for possession of ketamine and two cautions. Both these factors aggravate the offence.

The court will want to consider whether Rachel's remorse mitigates the offence.

It will be for the court to decide the extent of any adjustment but it is likely that the sentence would increase from the starting point. The court would likely

be concerned about Rachel's continuing use of ketamine and her vulnerability arising from her drug use. It is likely, therefore, that the court would impose a low-level community order for 12 months with a rehabilitative element.

Step three

There are no other factors indicating a reduction in sentence.

Step four

There is a guilty plea at the earliest opportunity, which should result in a reduction in sentence.

The likely sentence is a low-level community order for 12 months with a rehabilitative element.

Step five

The totality principle is not applicable here as it is a single offence.

Step six

Forfeiture and destruction of the drugs.

Step seven

The court should set out the reasons for its sentence.

Step eight

The defendant has been on unconditional bail so no adjustment for remand time is required.

Permitting premises to be used (Misuse of Drugs Act 1971 section 8)

Police officers visit a pub after neighbours complain of a strong smell of cannabis. The licensee of this pub is Peter. At the pub the police officers find a couple smoking cannabis in the smoking booth in the beer garden. Police find a joint and a bag containing 2g of cannabis. The couple admit that the cannabis is theirs and that they bought it on the high street before coming to the pub. In police interview, Peter admits allowing the cannabis to be smoked on his pub's premises, saying that business had been slow lately at the pub and he did not want to risk the loss of custom from the couple so had 'turned a blind eye'. Peter says that the couple were regulars and they had smoked at the pub once before. Peter said he did not think it was 'a big deal'. Peter is charged under section 8 of the Misuse of Drugs Act 1971 for permitting cannabis to be smoked on the premises of his pub. Peter has no previous convictions and pleads guilty.

Step one

The guideline for permitting premises to be used applies.

In terms of culpability, Peter had not taken an active role in supplying the cannabis to the couple and whilst he may have permitted use because he did not want to risk the loss of custom, there was no substantial financial gain expected or achieved in doing so.

The court would likely find Peter's culpability to be lower.

In terms of harm, there is no evidence that Peter has permitted cannabis to be smoked at his pub on a regular basis and the quantity of drugs found was no more than 3g. The court would likely find the harm to be lesser.

Lower culpability and lesser harm place the offence in category 3, which has a range of band A fine to a low-level community order with a starting point of a band C fine.

Step two

The presence of others in the pub, especially non-users, would aggravate the sentence.

There are no mitigating factors present.

It will be for the court to decide the extent of any adjustment, but it is likely that the sentence for this offence would be a band C fine.

Step three

There are no other factors indicating a reduction in sentence.

Step four

There is a guilty plea at the earliest opportunity, which should result in a reduction in sentence.

The likely sentence is a band C fine but the amount of the fine would be reduced.

Step five

The totality principle is not applicable here as it is a single offence.

Step six

Forfeiture and destruction of the drugs.

Step seven

The court should set out the reasons for its sentence.

Step eight

The defendant has been on unconditional bail so no adjustment for remand time is required.

Cultivation of cannabis plant (Misuse of Drugs Act 1971 section 6[2])

David's loft is searched by police and is found to contain four cannabis plants in a tent-like structure and some rudimentary equipment. David co-operated fully with the police and when interviewed about the plants, David told police they belonged to him and were for his own

personal use. He had bought the equipment off the Internet. He said he smoked a lot of cannabis and was unable to afford to buy cannabis so he decided to grow his own. David suffers from attention deficit disorder and began smoking cannabis at the age of 16 to help calm him down. David is now 23 and is determined to give up smoking cannabis, although he has not taken any demonstrable steps to do so. He has two previous convictions for possession of cannabis for which he received fines and pleads guilty at his first appearance at the magistrates' court.

Step one

The guideline for cultivation of cannabis plant applies.

In this case it is likely that the court will find the defendant to be in a lesser role as the cannabis grown was solely for his own use.

In terms of harm, it is likely that the court would regard it as category 4 since there are four cannabis plants involved.

Lesser role/category 4 has a range of a discharge to a medium-level community order. The starting point based on nine plants is a band C fine.

Step two

David has two previous convictions for possession of cannabis which aggravate the offence.

There would be a downward adjustment from the starting point to a band B fine, as the quantity is less than half the indicative quantity upon which the starting point is based. The court will also want to consider whether David's determination to address his addiction reflects personal mitigation, warranting a downward adjustment from the starting point. However, given his lack of demonstrable steps to do so, any adjustment would likely be limited.

It will be for the court to decide the extent of any adjustment but the court would likely consider that, in light of David's previous convictions and the previous lack of steps taken by him to address his addiction, the community threshold has been passed. Given David's current determination to address his drug addiction, the court may consider that a low-level community order with a drug rehabilitation requirement would be an appropriate sentence.

Step three

There are no other factors indicating a reduction in sentence.

Step four

There is a guilty plea at the earliest opportunity, which will lead to a reduction in the punitive elements of the community order.

The likely sentence is a low-level community order for 12 months with the following requirements:

1 Unpaid work: 40 hours.

2 Drug rehabilitation requirement.

Step five

The totality principle is not applicable here as it is a single offence.

Step six

Forfeiture and destruction of the drugs.

Step seven

The court should set out the reasons for its sentence.

Step eight

The defendant has been on unconditional bail so no adjustment for remand time is required.

⇨ The above information is reprinted with kind permission from the Sentencing Council. Visit http://sentencingcouncil.judiciary.gov.uk for more information on this and other related topics.

© Crown copyright

Deal or new deal? How the designer drugs trade impacts UK classification laws

Information from Nerditorial.

By Laura Hyde

Forty-two new designer drugs, billions of pounds spent on prohibition each year, and just one question – Is the UK Drugs Act still relevant to a modern society? While recent statistics show a significant reduction in overall drug use across the UK, many experts lambast the system, implying that drug classification is dictated by media hype rather than scientific analysis. This leaves many individuals calling for a reform, yet with an influx of legal highs arriving in Europe each year, and a government determined to make stringent cuts to the medicine, science and law enforcement resources, an overhaul may prove to be a complex undertaking.

Drug addiction has caused concern in the UK for over 50 years

Drug addiction has caused concern in the UK for over 50 years, but while studies illustrate that the nature of the drugs trade is constantly evolving, the prescribed antidote for the issue has remained largely unchanged since the drugs law was passed in 1971. When the number of controlled substances could be counted on an abacus, and prisons were furnished with Bibles instead of games consoles, the streamline three- tier system could be deemed a reasonable attempt to safeguard the general public from the dangers of substance abuse. Nowadays, due to the rapid advancement of technology, it is not only possible for consumers to find detailed drug information online, it is also possible for dealers to formulate their own legal substances which emulate the effects of illicit drugs. New substances are purchased via the Internet every day, and the current classification system simply cannot accommodate the high level of market growth, making it easy to manipulate. According to a recent report by the European Drugs and Drug Addiction Monitoring Centre, last year saw the emergence of 42 new narcotics in Britain, which is the highest amount ever to be recorded.

Under the current UK Drugs Act, the Government has limited weapons at their disposal when dealing with the problem. To ensure that fewer suspicious substances are absorbed into British culture, they could seek a blanket ban, effectively criminalising all 'designer' drugs, and classifying them according to the attributes of similar substances, but while such a decision might be seen to minimise the hazards associated with taking unknown drugs, the initiative would be difficult to sustain in light of plans to axe 34,000 police officers and make sentences for drugs mules more lenient. With the prospect of fewer law enforcement personnel and reduced jail time, the financial profit for criminals is likely to outweigh the risk of being incarcerated, causing many new narcotics to slip through the proverbial net.

Furthermore, even if a blanket ban were feasible, there is evidence to suggest that mere criminalisation is not always enough to reduce drug use by those on the club scene. According to an article in *The Guardian*, last year's controversial drug of choice, methedrone (or meow meow), remains as popular as cocaine, despite a high profile media campaign which resulted in the legal high being elevated to Class B. This casts doubt over whether classification systems actually protect those who discard health warnings and threats of confinement in the pursuit of a good time. One individual who rallied against the criminalisation of methedrone was Professor David Nutt, whose views on the classification law proved so unpopular that he was stripped of his position as chief drugs advisor to the Government in late 2009. In an interview with media, Nutt maintained that methedrone was not solely responsible for two teenage deaths, implying that more scientific research might have proved it to be a much safer alternative to cocaine.

> ## Even if a blanket ban were feasible, there is evidence to suggest that mere criminalisation is not always enough to reduce drug use

If this were proven correct, one option for drug control would be to allow scientists to analyse substances before any judicial decision is made, so that less toxic drugs could be offered to habitual users as a more appropriate substitute. Following the brutal cuts to the sciences and the NHS, it seems inconceivable that the Conservatives would want to 'waste' time and money on intense drug research, especially given the time it would take to complete studies, and the spectacular rate at which the latest trends take hold. Also, a single drug-related incident would give the media an opportunity to denigrate the programme among voters.

NERDITORIAL

Despite this, in countries where the drug-related mortality rate is low, such as the Netherlands, substance abuse is treated as a medical issue, and while the disciplinary system is still used for drug dealers and traffickers, rehabilitation is considered much more effective than incarceration for those who suffer from drug addiction. While it remains unlikely that the Conservatives will adopt a liberal drugs policy, removing drugs from the clutches of greedy criminals and into specialised clinics certainly has its advantages. Firstly, scientists would be able to conduct appropriate research, while users could use other low-level drugs until the safety of new ones had been properly assessed. If a drug is found to cause minimal harm, it can be added to the available selection, giving more choice to the consumer, and less control to the dealers which they otherwise must use to secure their fix. Equally, in a specialised environment, it would be easy for health professionals to track individual consumption levels and provide rehabilitation services to those who are considered overly dependent on narcotics. In this case, the law could concentrate on enforcing mandatory rehabilitation visits, with the threat

> *In countries where the drug-related mortality rate is low ... rehabilitation is considered much more effective than incarceration for those who suffer from drug addiction*

of punishment on the refusal to co-operate. This way, at least the Government could say they tried to curtail drug-related crime in a humanitarian way, rather than opting directly for stop and search, or a jail term which will probably result in more drug use.

In the end, it is necessary to realise this: recreational drug use has been around for a long time, and while popular trends will come and go with each generation, the temptation to experiment with substances is likely to remain, no matter how dangerous this may prove. If punishment becomes futile, then the only thing left to do is accept that people enjoy the level of escapism which some narcotics provide, and the drug trade will always be a criminal domain unless scientists are allowed to take control and investigate whether truly safe highs are a possibility. This, however, may be a difficult pill for David Cameron to swallow.

August 2011

⇨ The above information is reprinted with kind permission from Nerditorial. Visit www.nerditorial.com for further information.

> *Recreational drug use has been around for a long time, and while popular trends will come and go with each generation, the temptation to experiment with substances is likely to remain*

Drugs – time for better laws

Information from Release.

'Drugs – time for better laws' is Release's campaign to engage the public around the issue of drug policy. The failure of the current system is clear: it is time to stop criminalising tens of thousands of people in the UK every year – it is time for better laws.

On 2 June 2011, Release wrote to the Prime Minister calling for a review of the current drug policies, with a view to decriminalisation of possession for all drugs. This letter had been signed by leading QCs, three former Chief Constables, academics, politicians and high profile celebrities including Sting, Mike Leigh, Julie Christie and Kathy Burke.

We will be publishing a report on the state of decriminalisation around the world early in the New Year. We are also undertaking research into the disproportionate policing and prosecution of drug offences and how it impacts on BME communities, the young and those living in deprivation.

What can you do to support the campaign?

At the moment we are asking people to email the report of the Global Commission on Drug Policy to their MPs. The Home Affairs Select Committee has called for written evidence on the UK's drug policy as part of a major new enquiry. Interestingly, they have referenced the Global Commission on Drug Policy and appear to want to ask some of the questions we would like to see answered about the effectiveness of the current approach.

We are asking people to email their MP a copy of the report, which, among a series of recommendations, calls for decriminalisation. The Commissioners include Kofi Annan, Javier Solana and Richard Branson, as well as a host of other global figures. This has clearly influenced the Home Affairs Select Committee and we would hope it also influences other members of the House of Commons.

Please feel free to tweet and post to Facebook some of the reasons why:

Criminal records for drugs possession limits employment, education, travel

In the last ten years, nearly a million people have been convicted or cautioned for drug possession; the Misuse of Drugs Act 1971 was introduced 40 years ago this year, meaning that millions of people in the UK have been criminalised. This can be a barrier to employment, education and travel opportunities.

Portugal's decriminalisation of drug possession has seen fewer young people using drugs

Since the introduction of decriminalisation of drug possession in 2001, Portugal has seen a reduction in the number of young people taking drugs. This can be attributed to other factors but shows no causal link between decriminalisation and levels of drug use.

Harsh laws do not reduce drug use

The USA has one of the harshest legal systems for addressing drug use and yet has some of the highest drug use per capita on Earth.

If you are black in the UK you are nine times more likely to be stopped and searched for drugs

Portugal's decriminalisation of drug possession has seen less problematic drug use

Since the introduction of decriminalisation of drug possession in 2001, Portugal has seen a reduction in the number of problematic drug users.

Criminalising young people wastes their potential

Last year in England and Wales, nearly 30% of all cautions and prosecutions for drug possession were given to young people under the age of 21. This affects their future life opportunities.

Drug laws are discriminatory: black people nine times more likely to be stopped and searched

If you are black in the UK you are nine times more likely to be stopped and searched for drugs.

Drug laws are discriminatory: black people six times more likely to be arrested

If you are black in the UK you are six times more likely to be arrested for drug offences.

Drug laws are discriminatory: black people 11 times more likely to go to jail

If you are black in the UK you are 11 times more likely to be sent to prison for drug offences.

⇨ Information from Release: www.release.org.uk

© 2012 Release Legal Emergency & Drugs Service Ltd

Illegal drug use is in decline, NHS figures reveal

Fewer people of all ages are taking drugs such as cannabis, cocaine and heroin, according to survey.

By Denis Campbell, Health Correspondent

A generational shift away from drugs may be under way, addiction experts suggested today, as figures showed that illegal substances were declining in popularity among all age groups.

Fewer people in England and Wales are taking drugs such as cannabis, cocaine or heroin, according to an NHS survey, which confirmed that use was down in every age group from 11- to 59-year-olds. 20% of 16- to 25-year-olds used illegal drugs in 2009/10, down from 22.6% the year before, and well below the 29.7% recorded in 1996. Similarly, the proportion of 11- to 15-year-olds who have ever used a banned substance has fallen from 29% in 2001 to 22% last year.

The survey found 8.6% of those aged 16 to 59, or 2.8 million people, were using illicit substances in 2009/10 – the lowest ever figure since drug-taking trends were first monitored in 1996, down from 10.1% in 2008/09, 11.1% in 1996 and the record 12.3% in 2003/04.

The proportion using Class A drugs such as heroin or crack also fell year-on-year (3.7% to 3.1%), as did those taking cannabis (7.9% to 6.6%).

The findings were contained in the NHS Information Centre's annual survey of drugs misuse in England. It combines official sources of information on drug trends with extensive interviews with the public about their own habits to identify patterns of self-reported substance usage.

Drug experts welcomed the decline and cited the recession, the declining popularity of smoking 'skunk' cannabis, which is proving too strong for some users, and greater knowledge among young people about the potential harms of drugs as possible explanations.

'There could well be a generational shift away from drugs going on,' said Martin Barnes, Chief Executive of DrugScope, which represents drug treatment services across the UK.

'Overall drug use has been declining significantly over the last six or seven years, which is encouraging, and we are seeing fewer young people reporting that they are using drugs. It could be to do with young people's culture and fashion, that they are more aware of the fact they could do themselves harm by taking drugs. It's a fair supposition that at least some young people are a bit more savvy about the downsides of drugs.

'It may be that they see such substances as "mucky drugs",' added Barnes.

Although more marijuana is now being produced in 'cannabis factories' in the UK, an increasing amount is skunk, which is two to three times stronger than traditional cannabis resin. 'For some users the experience [with skunk] can be too powerful or unpleasant or unpredictable for their liking.'

However, other trends in drug use showed no room for complacency, he said. 'Other shifts in behaviour, such as people experimenting with a wider range of drugs than before, or combining different drugs with alcohol, are of concern because they are hazardous patterns.'

The Department of Health welcomed the decline. 'Today's publication provides some very good news – drug misuse is falling in all age groups. But there is still much more to do.'

8.6% of those aged 16 to 59, or 2.8 million people, were using illicit substances in 2009/10

Anne Milton, the Public Health Minister, stressed that getting people off drugs completely was the Government's key aim and that the planned new NHS agency Public Health England would work towards that.

Simon Antrobus, Chief Executive of the drugs and alcohol charity Addaction, said: 'While the overall figures are certainly encouraging, it's no time to get complacent. Drug use remains a big problem in this country, and specialist services remain vital in tackling it.'

The greater availability of support and treatment for users may help explain the falls, he said. 'Between 2009 and 2010, Addaction saw a 67% increase in the numbers helped by our services for under-25s, for example. More people are getting help for their problems – a great thing.'

However, today's report also found that the numbers of admissions to hospital due to drug problems rose last year, up 5.7% to 44,585. And some 206,889 people received help from drug services for drug dependency. Of 62,685 who underwent treatment, 38% kicked their habit, researchers found.

27 January 2011

THE GUARDIAN

Call for action on 'legal high' drugs

Information from NHS Choices.

Government drug advisers have today called for tighter regulation of 'legal highs' – recreational drugs sold legally due to loopholes in the law. In a new report the Advisory Council on the Misuse of Drugs (ACMD) has published details of how drugs such as 'meow meow' (mephedrone), which was banned last year, have been openly sold over the Internet under the guise of being 'plant food' or 'research chemicals'.

The report also highlighted the false perception that just because a drug is technically legal it must be safe, pointing out that there have been at least 42 deaths associated with the use of mephedrone, and dozens more where its use has been suspected.

While the mephedrone family of drugs has now been banned, the ACMD said those manufacturing legal highs are increasingly tweaking the chemical formulas of banned legal highs to bypass bans on specific substances. In response, it suggested that legislation should be used to make it illegal to produce substances with similar effects to banned drugs, rather than just banning specific chemicals as they emerge.

In its report, the ACMD made further recommendations aimed at trying to reduce sales, demand and harms.

He said the 'stuff' was legal, so it was safe to take!

What are legal highs?

Legal highs are drugs that are intended to mimic the effects of illegal drugs but can technically be sold or possessed legally. However, the lack of legal control does not imply that they are safe, and a number of substances sold as legal highs in the past have since been associated with health problems and even death. For example, until it was banned in 2010, the substance mephedrone (also known as meow meow) was legally allowed to be sold when labelled as a research chemical or as a plant food. However, recent data has shown that despite perceptions it was safe, the drug has contributed to at least 42 recorded deaths. Its use has also been suspected in dozens of further deaths.

While many substances that were once sold as legal highs have since been banned, the ACMD says that chemists are constantly using their knowledge to develop new 'legal highs' that fall outside existing drug legislation. These are often chemically similar to banned substances and produce similar effects, but due to them having different chemical compositions they may not technically be governed by existing laws. Given the new, or novel, nature of legal highs, the ACMD refers to them as Novel Psychoactive Substances (NPS).

The ACMD says legal highs generally fall into four broad categories:

⇨ products with names that give no indication of what they contain;

⇨ substances that are designed to be similar to specific controlled drugs;

⇨ substances related to medicines;

⇨ herbal or fungal materials or their extracts.

NPS products cannot be marketed, sold or labelled as being intended for human consumption, which would make them subject to strict pharmaceutical legislation. To circumvent these laws they are often labelled as something else; for example, plant food, bath salts, research chemical or boat cleaner, with disclaimers saying they are 'not for human consumption'.

What issues did the report consider?

The report considered a number of different factors relating to NPS, their use and measures to tackle them.

Among the specific issues examined were:

⇨ legal highs' place in the UK drug scene;

⇨ personal harm;

⇨ societal impact;

NHS CHOICES

- ⇨ measures to reduce demand;
- ⇨ measures to reduce supply;
- ⇨ current and future legislation;
- ⇨ ways to future-proof drug laws.

The ACMD was keen to point out that the report does not provide a solution to the current problem or guidance on specific NPS products, but rather options that may help reduce the harmful impact of legal highs. However, in considering the issue in general, the report described cases studies for mephedrone, which was banned in 2010, and Ivory Wave (also known as desoxypipradrol or 2-DPMP), an NPS that has not yet been classified as a controlled substance.

Chemists are constantly using their knowledge to develop new 'legal highs' that fall outside existing drug legislation

In the case of mephedrone the report highlighted how quickly the novel drug rose in popularity, but also that there has been a growing number of adverse incidents reported, and at least 42 deaths where the drug played a significant role. The report also stated that a few months after mephedrone was banned, those manufacturing legal highs started producing a similar (and technically legal) substance called naphyrone, highlighting how quickly existing laws can be circumvented.

Desoxypipradrol, the main active ingredient in Ivory Wave, is not yet a 'controlled substance' (illegal to supply or possess), although its import into this country has been banned. However, testing of Ivory Wave products has shown its chemical contents can vary, and at times it may contain controlled substances. This means that a person who had bought an Ivory Wave product thinking it was legal could still be subject to prosecution if they were stopped by the police and found to be carrying a controlled substance.

What are the dangers from using legal highs?

Generally, there is a lack of safety data on the legal highs, which mostly appear to be untested and unregulated compounds. Aside from these obvious risks, the contents of products are often variable and not specified on packaging, meaning people can never be sure exactly what they are taking, even if they have used a product before.

Even though there is limited data available on these substances, there appears to have been an increase in hospital admissions and medical appointments due to the toxicity of legal highs. In addition, health services are starting to see health problems caused by regular use of legal highs, including dependence that requires detoxification treatment.

Across all adults surveyed (ages 16–59), 1.4% had used mephedrone in the past 12 months, a similar level of usage to ecstasy

Testing has also shown that many NPS are synthetic amphetamine-like stimulants, meaning they are likely to share many of the well-documented adverse effects of amphetamines, such as dependence. It also means that it is possible that the more potent NPS are likely to carry an overdose risk at just a few milligrams, which is likely to be associated with acute toxic effects.

How popular are legal highs?

The ACMD says that NPS use is such a new phenomenon that it is hard to gauge how popular and readily available these substances are. However, while the council says that robust data on the issue is often unavailable, sources such as the British Crime Survey have recently started collecting data on their use. The council highlights some of the survey's data on mephedrone for 2010/11, which suggested that:

- ⇨ 4.4% of people aged 16–24 had used mephedrone in the past 12 months, the same proportion that had used cocaine. (This data related to both the period when mephedrone was considered to be a legal high and when it became a controlled substance and was banned.)

- ⇨ Across all adults surveyed (ages 16–59), 1.4% had used mephedrone in the past 12 months, a similar level of usage to ecstasy.

The report also cited a 2011 survey run by the dance music magazine *Mixmag*, which asked clubbers several question on their use of drugs. Although the survey was aimed specifically at clubbers, 75% of them said it was easy or very easy to obtain mephedrone prior to the ban. Post-ban, 38% of respondents said it was easy or very easy to obtain. The same survey, however, said that 42% of respondents had tried the drug pre-ban, but that 61% had tried it post-ban.

The ACMD report noted that *British Crime Survey* figures suggested that overall drug use is coming down in the UK.

What recommendations does the council make?

The report made extensive recommendations relating to policy, the law, public health messages and how to close loopholes that mean that drugs are legal until they are specifically deemed controlled substances. Some suggested measures recommend that:

⇨ The UK should develop EU and international networks to address the issue of legal highs.

⇨ Countries involved in the manufacture of the legal highs should be encouraged to stop.

⇨ The UK Government should put in place processes that would allow the Misuse of Drugs Act 1971 to be updated quickly and easily when minor changes are required.

⇨ Chemical detection and testing methods need to be developed so that illegal compounds present in legal highs can be easily detected.

⇨ That new legislation should be considered, possibly similar to the Analogue Act 1986 used in the US. This would mean that chemical substances similar to controlled chemicals would automatically be banned, that is, it would automatically be illegal to create a chemical with similar properties to a banned substance.

⇨ The burden of proof should be placed upon the supplier to establish beyond reasonable doubt that the product being sold is not for human consumption and is safe for its intended use – in other words, to prevent it being marketed as bath salts or plant food.

Countries involved in the manufacture of the legal highs should be encouraged to stop

---

⇨ Specific legislation, namely the Consumer Protection from Unfair Trading Regulation and General Product Safety Regulations (2005), should be applied to the sale of legal highs, and the Advertising Standards Agency should investigate claims made by the websites selling legal highs.

⇨ Research into the chemistry, pharmacology, toxicity and social harm of legal highs should be increased.

⇨ Moves to increase public awareness should be implemented.

October 2011

⇨ Reproduced by kind permission of the Department of Health – nhs.uk.

NHS CHOICES

Getting tough on drugs just doesn't work

Britain's drug policy has failed. It's time for a radical overhaul.

By Dr Julian Huppert MP

The failure of Britain's drugs policy is blatantly obvious. Traffickers and dealers are making huge amounts of money through drugs coming into this country and, as a result of our growing drugs problem, we are facing enormous health issues. I believe the time has come for us to radically overhaul our approach to the drugs problem, which is growing on an international scale.

It is time that we developed a rational policy based on scientific evidence rather than on media hype

Taking a tough line through the courts and imposing jail sentences on drug addicts for relatively small drugs charges hasn't worked. Our jails are overcrowded. Drugs have become more accessible, making more money for the traffickers and dealers. In turn, more and more people are using illegal substances, often turning to crime to fuel their habits. New substances are coming onto the market and our young people are experimenting with the so-called 'party drugs', sometimes with tragic results. We are facing a vicious circle while at the same time continuing with laws which are, for the most part, ineffective.

We cannot continue in this way; we have to find a new approach. The drugs market is changing and the Government must respond to that change. It is time that we developed a rational policy based on scientific evidence rather than on media hype. I have been working as vice-chair of the all-party parliamentary group on drug policy reform to generate ideas and led a debate on the issue at the Lib Dem autumn conference designed to open up discussion.

But I don't know what the correct solution is. I do know that something has to change and we can no longer rely on a policy which isn't working and hasn't worked for decades. The Prime Minister, David Cameron, acknowledged this recently and accepted that we need to find a better way based on education and treatment. But we cannot do this without expert help and we need to seek expert advice so that we can find out what is and isn't working and look at all our options.

I believe we need a policy which provides treatment for addicts so that we can help them kick their drug habits without adding to their problems. We need to provide better education so that our young people can make informed choices. We need a policy that concentrates resources on the serious issue of drug dealing and trafficking and allows the police to concentrate their efforts on tackling organised drug pushers and gangs. And we need a policy that doesn't add to our already overcrowded prisons which are putting an increasing burden on public finances.

How we do that is not simple, and there is no simple answer – I'm certainly not calling for immediate legalisation of drugs.

Whatever we do, we must take this slowly, looking at all the options open to us so that we make sure we get it right. We have to move on this debate and we can only do that if we have independent expert analysis which can help to show us the way forward. I believe that to do nothing and continue to pursue drugs policies which are ineffective and expensive is no longer an option.

Dr Julian Huppert has been Liberal Democrat MP for Cambridge since 2010

27 July 2011

⇨ The above information is reprinted with kind permission from Politics.co.uk.

© SquareDigitalMedia Ltd

POLITICS.CO.UK

⇨ Of the general adult population aged 16–59, around ten million people, or 30%, say they have ever tried an illegal drug. The figure drops to around 10% for use in the last year and just over 5% for use in the last month. (page 1)

⇨ In 2009, coroners deemed that the deaths of 2,182 people in the UK were drug-related. (page 2)

⇨ Recreational drugs can be classified as stimulants, depressants and hallucinogens. Some drugs, however, can overlap these categories: for example, ecstasy is both a stimulant and a hallucinogen. (page 3)

⇨ More drug services are seeing people coming forward for help with the drug ketamine, according to DrugScope's 2011 *Street Drug Trends Survey*. (page 5)

⇨ According to widespread research by DrugScope, dangerous party drug ketamine has a legal doppelganger in the form of methoxetamine (MXE) or 'Mexxy', which mimics the effects of ketamine. (page 6)

⇨ Volatile substances are depressants which slow down the activity of the brain and central nervous system. (page 7)

⇨ More than one in three (35%) of 25- to 34-year-olds agree or strongly agree with the statement 'experimenting with cannabis is a normal part of growing up'. (page 8)

⇨ One recent study found that 70% of pupils couldn't recall any drug education in their secondary school. (page 11)

⇨ Each individual will be affected in different ways by the same drug and the same amount of the drug. (page 12)

⇨ Estimates of the number of heroin and crack users in England fell from a peak of 332,000 in 2005/07 to 306,000 in 2009/10. (page 13)

⇨ Research shows that crimes committed by drug users are halved when they are in treatment. (page 16)

⇨ 28,000 adults left drug treatment free from dependency in 2010/11 – a 150% increase on the figure for 2005/06. (page 17)

⇨ Of the 255,556 adult drug users who entered treatment for the first time between 2005 and 2011, 28% (71,887) left free of dependency and have not returned since. (page 18)

⇨ Drugs include a broad range of substances, ranging from prescription medicines, to illegal street drugs such as cocaine and ecstasy, to readily available products such as tobacco and alcohol. (page 21)

⇨ The Sentencing Council for England and Wales published new sentencing guidelines for drug offences which came into force from February 2012. (page 22)

⇨ Drugs in Class A include cocaine, ecstasy, LSD, magic mushrooms, heroin and methadone. (page 24)

⇨ Recent statistics show a significant reduction in overall drug use across the UK. (page 32)

⇨ If you are black in the UK you are 11 times more likely to be sent to prison for drug offences. (page 34)

⇨ Fewer people in England and Wales are taking drugs such as cannabis, cocaine or heroin, according to an NHS survey, which confirmed that use was down in every age group from 11- to 59-year-olds. (page 35)

⇨ A recent ACMD report highlighted the false perception that just because a drug is technically legal it must be safe, pointing out that there have been at least 42 deaths associated with the use of mephedrone. (page 36)

⇨ 4.4% of people aged 16–24 surveyed had used mephedrone in the past 12 months. (page 37)

Addiction

A dependence on a substance which makes it very difficult to stop taking it. Addiction can be either physical, meaning the user's body has become dependent on the substance and will suffer negative symptoms if the substance is withdrawn, or psychological, meaning a user has no physical need to take a substance, but will experience strong cravings if it is withdrawn.

Amphetamines

Synthetic drugs which can be swallowed, inhaled or injected. Their effects can include increased mental alertness, energy and confidence. Most amphetamines are Class B substances, but crystal meth and prepared-for-injection speed are Class A. Taking amphetamines can cause anxiety or paranoia and risks include overdose and psychological dependence. They can also put strain on a user's heart, leading to cardiac problems.

Dealing

Supplying drugs to another person, usually in return for money. However, giving drugs away free to friends is also classed as dealing, and is subject to the same penalties as selling drugs. Dealing illegal drugs carries greater penalties than possession for personal use.

Depressant

A substance that slows down the nervous system, making the user feel calmer and more relaxed. These drugs are also known as 'downers' and include alcohol, heroin and tranquillisers.

Drug

A chemical that alters the way the mind and body works. Legal drugs include alcohol, tobacco, caffeine and prescription medicines taken for medical reasons. Illegal drugs taken for recreation include cannabis, cocaine, ecstasy and speed. These illegal substances are divided into three classes – A, B and C – according to the danger they pose to the user and to society (with A being the most harmful and C the least).

Hallucinogen

A drug which produces visions and sensations detached from reality (a 'trip'). Common hallucinogens include LSD, ketamine and magic mushrooms.

Misuse of Drugs Act 1971

Legislation prohibiting the use of dangerous recreational substances, making it an offence to possess banned drugs for personal use or with the intent to supply. It also divides drugs into three classes according to the degree of harm they pose to the individual and to society – A, B or C – each with different associated penalties.

Opiate

Drugs made from the opium poppy, such as heroin, opium and morphine. Methadone is a synthetic opioid: a man-made substance designed to act on the same opioid receptors as morphine and heroin. It is often used to treat people with a dependency on these substances.

Overdose

This occurs when an individual takes such a large dose of a drug that their body cannot cope with the effects. An overdose can cause organ failure, coma and death.

Reclassification

When an illegal substance is moved from one drugs class into another, after its harmfulness has been reassessed or new research has uncovered previously-unknown negative effects. Cannabis has been reclassified twice in the past decade, being moved from Class B to Class C in 2004 and back to Class B again in 2009.

Stimulant

A substance that speeds up the nervous system, making people feel more alert or energised. These drugs are also known as 'uppers' and include caffeine, cocaine, ecstasy and speed.

Solvent

A volatile substance which gives off fumes. Vapours from products including paint, glue and aerosols can be inhaled and cause intoxication. Volatile substance abuse is highly dangerous, killing more children aged ten to 15 than all illegal drugs put together.

Withdrawal

The symptoms that occur when a person stops taking a drug they are physically dependent on, making the person feel ill and suffer flu-like symptoms.

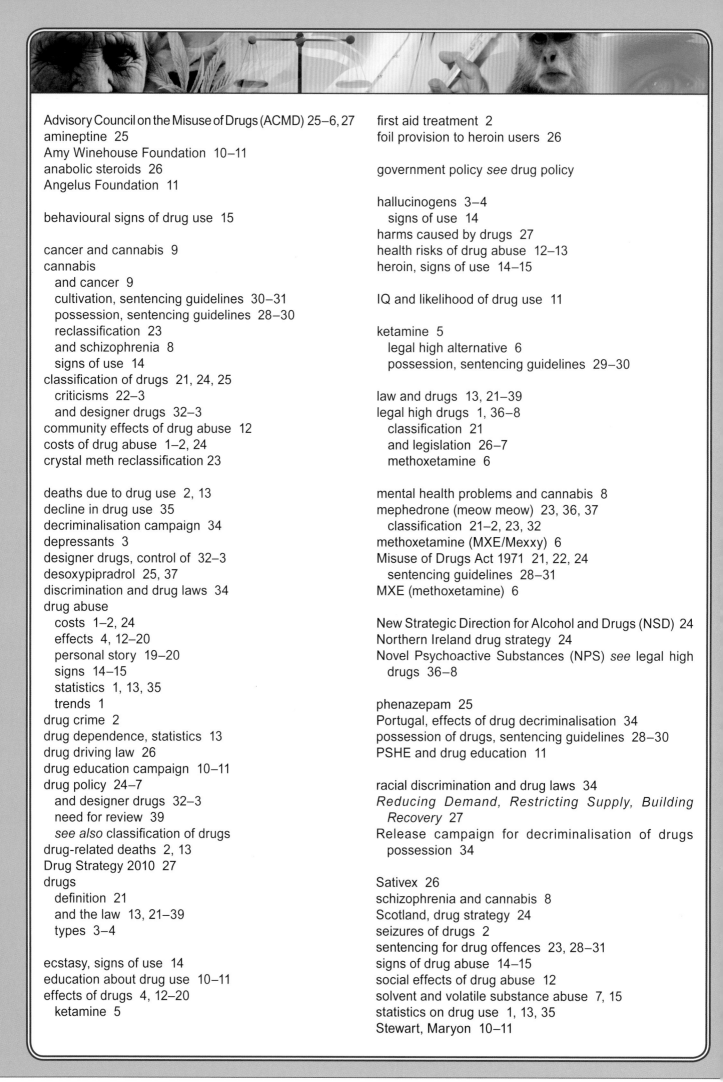

Advisory Council on the Misuse of Drugs (ACMD) 25–6, 27
amineptine 25
Amy Winehouse Foundation 10–11
anabolic steroids 26
Angelus Foundation 11

behavioural signs of drug use 15

cancer and cannabis 9
cannabis
  and cancer 9
  cultivation, sentencing guidelines 30–31
  possession, sentencing guidelines 28–30
  reclassification 23
  and schizophrenia 8
  signs of use 14
classification of drugs 21, 24, 25
  criticisms 22–3
  and designer drugs 32–3
community effects of drug abuse 12
costs of drug abuse 1–2, 24
crystal meth reclassification 23

deaths due to drug use 2, 13
decline in drug use 35
decriminalisation campaign 34
depressants 3
designer drugs, control of 32–3
desoxypipradrol 25, 37
discrimination and drug laws 34
drug abuse
  costs 1–2, 24
  effects 4, 12–20
  personal story 19–20
  signs 14–15
  statistics 1, 13, 35
  trends 1
drug crime 2
drug dependence, statistics 13
drug driving law 26
drug education campaign 10–11
drug policy 24–7
  and designer drugs 32–3
  need for review 39
  see also classification of drugs
drug-related deaths 2, 13
Drug Strategy 2010 27
drugs
  definition 21
  and the law 13, 21–39
  types 3–4

ecstasy, signs of use 14
education about drug use 10–11
effects of drugs 4, 12–20
  ketamine 5

first aid treatment 2
foil provision to heroin users 26

government policy see drug policy

hallucinogens 3–4
  signs of use 14
harms caused by drugs 27
health risks of drug abuse 12–13
heroin, signs of use 14–15

IQ and likelihood of drug use 11

ketamine 5
  legal high alternative 6
  possession, sentencing guidelines 29–30

law and drugs 13, 21–39
legal high drugs 1, 36–8
  classification 21
  and legislation 26–7
  methoxetamine 6

mental health problems and cannabis 8
mephedrone (meow meow) 23, 36, 37
  classification 21–2, 23, 32
methoxetamine (MXE/Mexxy) 6
Misuse of Drugs Act 1971 21, 22, 24
  sentencing guidelines 28–31
MXE (methoxetamine) 6

New Strategic Direction for Alcohol and Drugs (NSD) 24
Northern Ireland drug strategy 24
Novel Psychoactive Substances (NPS) see legal high
  drugs 36–8

phenazepam 25
Portugal, effects of drug decriminalisation 34
possession of drugs, sentencing guidelines 28–30
PSHE and drug education 11

racial discrimination and drug laws 34
Reducing Demand, Restricting Supply, Building
  Recovery 27
Release campaign for decriminalisation of drugs
  possession 34

Sativex 26
schizophrenia and cannabis 8
Scotland, drug strategy 24
seizures of drugs 2
sentencing for drug offences 23, 28–31
signs of drug abuse 14–15
social effects of drug abuse 12
solvent and volatile substance abuse 7, 15
statistics on drug use 1, 13, 35
Stewart, Maryon 10–11

stimulants 3
  signs of use 14
substitute prescribing 16
supply of drugs, sentencing guidelines 28–9

tapentadol 25
temporary class drug orders 25
treatment
  for drug dependency 16–18
  emergency treatment 2

Unwin, Vicky 10–11

Wales, drug strategy 24
Winehouse, Amy 10
workplace, signs of drug misuse 15

young people and drug misuse 1
  treatment 17

ACKNOWLEDGEMENTS

The publisher is grateful for permission to reproduce the following material.

While every care has been taken to trace and acknowledge copyright, the publisher tenders its apology for any accidental infringement or where copyright has proved untraceable. The publisher would be pleased to come to a suitable arrangement in any such case with the rightful owner.

Chapter One: Illegal Drugs in the UK

Overview of the UK drug scene, © 2012 DrugScope, *If someone has taken drugs...,*© Surgery Door, *Drugs,* © 2012 University of Cambridge Counselling Service, *Ketamine problems on the rise,* © DrugScope, *'Safe ketamine': experts warn over trend for 'legal high' drug,* © The Huffington Post UK, *Introduction to solvent and volatile substance abuse,* © 2011 Re-Solv, *Cannabis and schizophrenia,* © Rethink Mental Illness, *'Cannabis cure for brain cancer' headline is misleading,* © Cancer Research UK, *Amy Winehouse's death prompts compulsory drug education in schools campaign,* © Press Association, *Clever children more likely to take drugs,* © The British Psychological Society.

Chapter Two: The Effects of Drug Abuse

The effects and impacts of drugs, © 2011 Public Health Agency, Northern Ireland, *Dependent drug users,* © National Treatment Agency for Substance Misuse, *How to recognise drug abuse,* © 2010 Public Health Agency, Northern Ireland, *Drug treatment in England: the road to recovery,* © National Treatment Agency for Substance Misuse, *'The story of what made me who I am',* © Wired in Ltd 2011.

Chapter Three: Drugs and the Law

Illegal drug use in the UK, © Square Digital Media Ltd, *Drug policy: legislation, strategies and economic analysis,* © Crown copyright is reproduced with the permission of Her Majesty's Stationery Office, *Sentencing guideline for drug offences comes into force,* © Crown copyright is reproduced with the permission of Her Majesty's Stationery Office, *Deal or new deal? How the designer drugs trade impacts UK classification laws,* © Nerditorial, *Drugs – time for better laws,* © 2012 Release Legal Emergency & Drugs Service Ltd, *Illegal drug use is in decline, NHS figures reveal,* © Guardian News & Media Ltd 2011, *Call for action on 'legal high' drugs,* © Crown copyright is reproduced with the permission of Her Majesty's Stationery Office, *Getting tough on drugs just doesn't work,* © SquareDigitalMedia Ltd.

Illustrations

Pages 1, 10, 21, 38: Don Hatcher; pages 4, 13, 31, 36: Angelo Madrid; pages 6, 20, 33, 39: Simon Kneebone; pages 7, 16: Bev Aisbett.

Cover photography

Left: © Rik Schutte. Centre: © Alex Madyart. Right: © Adam Ciesielski.

Additional acknowledgements

Research by Carolyn Kirby.

Editorial on behalf of Independence Educational Publishers by Cara Acred.

With thanks to the Independence team: Mary Chapman, Sandra Dennis and Jan Sunderland.

Lisa Firth
Cambridge
April, 2012

ASSIGNMENTS

The following tasks aim to help you think through the debate surrounding substance abuse and provide a better understanding of the topic.

1 According to the 2010/2011 'British Crime Survey', ketamine use has almost doubled since 2007. Using the Internet, research the side-effects of ketamine, its history in UK legislation and why it has risen in popularity. Write a summary of your findings.

2 Design a poster to discourage solvent and volatile substance abuse, outlining its dangerous side-effects.

3 Using the Guardian newspaper website, find the full data report from their 'Global Drugs Survey 2012'. Write a blog post summarising these findings and create a set of graphs to accompany your article.

4 Read the article *Clever children more likely to take drugs* on page 11. The British Psychological Society state that this finding is a correlation and that they can't say that higher IQ causes drug use. In small groups, think about environmental factors that might explain why clever children are more likely to take drugs. Compare your findings with other groups.

5 Watch the film 'Trainspotting'. Is its portrayal of heroin addicts in 90s Edinburgh still relevant to the UK today? Think about the effect that drug abuse has on the characters' relationships, health and lifestyle. Write a review of the film.

6 Plan a website that will provide worried parents with advice and information about drugs. Sections could include physical and behavioural signs of drug use, common street drugs and their side-effects, and advice on how parents can help their children. Write the text for at least three key sections and think of a name and logo for the site.

7 Create a storyboard for a TV ad campaign that will highlight the legal consequences of drug use. The campaign should be aimed at teenagers and explain the penalties for using Class A, B and C drugs. Most importantly, it should demonstrate the long-term impact that a criminal record could have on their lives.

8 Do you think binge drinking is a more serious problem than illegal drug use in the UK? Why is drinking more socially acceptable than drug taking? List your thoughts and then discuss with a partner.

9 How effective do you think drugs education lessons are in schools? How could drugs education be improved?

10 Research the history of legal and illegal drug use in Britain, from the 16th century to the present day. Have dangerous drugs such as opium always been illegal? Which drug do you think has done the most harm during Britain's history? Create an illustrated timeline showing the status of drugs in law and society through the ages.

11 Is cannabis a 'gateway drug', leading young people on to try harder drugs such as ecstasy and cocaine? In groups, role play a radio talk show discussing this issue, taking on the roles of parents, teenagers, experts and campaigners.

12 Read *'The story of what made me who I am'* on pages 19-20. Write a diary entry covering one day in Iain's life as he struggles to recover from his drug addiction and get clean for good.

13 In pairs, role play a conversation between a parent and their teenage child about cannabis use. The parent has used cannabis in their own youth but is concerned that modern strains of 'skunk' are much stronger than the cannabis resin of 20 years' ago. Their teenager feels the parent is preaching at them to 'do as I say, not as I did'. How might each get their point across?

14 'This house believes that drugs should be legalised so that creation and use can be carefully regulated, with profits taken away from the dealers and put back into society.' Debate this motion as a class, with one half arguing in favour and the other against.

15 Find out about a high-profile death associated with drug use, such as that of Leah Betts in 1995, Rachel Whitear in 2000 or Louise Cattell in 2011. What impact did it have? Write a summary of the tragedy and the campaign which followed.